Church, Ministry and Unity

Faith and the Future
General Editor: David Nicholls

Choices
Ethics and the Christian
David Brown

Church and Nation
Peter Cornwell

Pastoral Care and the Parish
Peter Davie

The Faith Abroad
John D. Davies

Church, Ministry and Unity
A Divine Commission
James E. Griffiss

The Authority of Divine Love
Richard Harries

The Bible
Fountain and Well of Truth
John Muddiman

Faith, Prayer and Devotion
Ralph Townsend

Sacraments and Liturgy
The Outward Signs
Louis Weil

Church, Ministry and Unity

A Divine Commission

James E. Griffiss

Basil Blackwell

First published 1983
Basil Blackwell Publisher Limited
108 Cowley Road, Oxford OX4 1JF, England

British Library Cataloguing in Publication Data
Griffiss, James E.
    Church, ministry and unity. − (Faith and the future)
    1. Christian union
    I. Title   II. Series
    262'.72   BX8.2

    ISBN 0-631-13185-X
    ISBN 0-631-13227-9   Pbk

Typeset by Cambrian Typesetters
Aldershot, Hants
Printed in Great Britain by T.J. Press Ltd, Padstow

Contents

Foreword

This book is one of a series whose writers consider some important aspects of Christianity in the contemporary scene and in so doing draw inspiration from the Catholic revival in the Anglican Communion which began in Oxford one hundred and fifty years ago. This revival — with its thinkers, pastors, prophets, social reformers and not a few who have been held to be saints — has experienced changes in the understanding of the Christian faith since the time of the Tractarians and has none the less borne witness to themes which are deep and unchanging. Among these are the call to holiness, the communion of saints, the priesthood of the Church and its ministers and a sacramental religion, both otherworldly and with revolutionary claims upon man's social life.

I am myself convinced that the renewal of the Church for today and tomorrow needs a deep recovery of these themes of Catholic tradition and a vision of their contemporary application. The books of this series are designed towards this end, and I am sure that readers will be grateful for the help they give. Many are thirsty but 'the well is deep'.

+ Michael Ramsey

1 Christ and the Church: the Heritage of the Oxford Movement

In the gospel accounts of the life and work of Jesus of Nazareth one question is asked over and over again: Who is this man who can do and say things which demand our attention and call for our response? In what is called the Confession of Peter (Luke 9:18–21), the question is put by Jesus himself: Who do people say that I am? Who do you say that I am? Peter answers: You are the Christ, the Son of the living God. Elsewhere in the gospels the question is called forth by the authority Jesus has over the lives of other people, by his words and actions of mercy and judgement, by his miracles, and finally by his death and resurrection. Indeed, the whole of the New Testament can be understood as containing many different attempts to answer the question put by the words, deeds, and events which surround that strange and enigmatic figure. And the great majority of people who have believed in him throughout the centuries of Christianity have found themselves faced with the same question, and have been compelled to answer it in some form or other. Jesus Christ is at the centre of Christian faith; who he is and what his authority means for us remain even now the central question of our belief in him.

The answers given to that question have been many and various. They have reflected the times and circumstances, the philosophy and culture, of those who have attempted to answer it; and they have, certainly, reflected the particular experience of him as saviour and lord which people have had in their individual lives. Just as the writers of the New Testament sought the answers, so in other periods of the Church's history the bishops and pastors of the community, theologians, lay people, poets and painters have struggled to find adequate ways to express what they believe about him, that are adequate to their own experience of him and that of the community to which they belong, and adequate also to tell the story of Jesus to others as honestly and completely as they can. From time to time it has been necessary for the Church to say that certain ways of talking about Jesus, certain ways of telling the story of his saving work in the lives of those who believe, are less than adequate, less than faithful to what Christians as a community of faith have known of him in their history. Out of that long history of controversy and accord, of experiencing the reality of Jesus Christ and of telling his story, has emerged what Christians now call the doctrine of the Incarnation. It is true that some of the ways in which that doctrine about Jesus Christ and our faith in him has been expressed can be called into question by biblical and theological scholars, but it is also true that what it is attempting to express remains fundamental to Christian belief, not only to our belief about who Jesus is, but also how Christians understand their own lives in relation to the God about whom Jesus spoke and whom in some profound way he represents. The doctrine of the Incarnation is important, whatever difficulties it may present to us today, because now as in the past it expresses the central belief which has structured and formed the life of the community which believes in Jesus, and so enables those who believe to reflect more deeply on the nature and purpose of that community. In other words, the doctrine of the Incarnation is a continuing attempt to understand and to express who Jesus is, who those who believe in him are, and who the God is of whom he speaks.

At the time of the Oxford Movement in the Church of England, the doctrine of the Incarnation became of profound importance in structuring and forming the way in which people thought about the Church and the Christian life. So much has been written about the history of the Oxford Movement, from its beginning in 1833 when John Keble preached the Assize Sermon to its end − or better its transformation – with the departure of J.H. Newman and others to the Church of Rome in the forties, that little needs to be recounted here. The publication of the Tracts for the Times, the other writings of Newman, Keble and Pusey, the significant theological work of Robert Wilberforce, and the almost endless controversies and trials are well known, even though much of it may seem strange to us now. What is evident in the Tractarians' writings – tracts, sermons, historical studies and personal correspondence – is their belief in Jesus Christ as incarnate lord. That belief more than anything else motivated and inspired them and created for people of the Church of England and for Anglicans elsewhere in the world a new and more dynamic understanding of the Church, of themselves, and of their mission. The heritage which Anglicans of today have received from the Oxford Movement is deeply grounded in the belief that Jesus Christ comes to us with a unique authority and calling to holiness, and that the Church which believes in him must carry out that belief in every aspect of its life and work. The central theme of this study of the Oxford Movement and its contribution to the way in which Anglicans still understand the Church and themselves will be, therefore, the doctrine of the Incarnation: how that doctrine has been a major concern for them as they have reflected upon who they are in the larger Christian community and what their particular calling and mission to the One Church of Christ may be. The leaders of the Oxford Movement believed and taught that the Church of England was part of the One, Holy, Catholic and Apostolic Church which has existed through the ages; and they could believe that because of what they believed about Jesus Christ as incarnate lord. In this first chapter, then, I want to say something about what speaking about Jesus Christ in that way means, and why it is important for an understanding of the Church and the Christian life.

Faith in Jesus Christ has led Christian people to make some very strong claims, even difficult ones, about that enigmatic figure who comes to us in the words of the New Testament.

3

In the historical terms we would use about other figures of the past, we know comparatively little about him: that he was an obscure, itinerant preacher who performed some wondrous acts; a member of a small nation who finally was crucified because his teaching and activities were unsettling to those in power. Beginning with the New Testament itself, however, what Christian faith has claimed about him is much more than that. It has claimed that he was raised from the dead by the power of God, that he is lord and saviour of all creation, that he is one with the transcendent mystery that human beings call God, and that he is present to the world now through his Spirit. None of those claims can be demonstrated in the categories and through the methods which we use to deal with the world of our everyday experience; indeed, they have from time to time been rejected or modified in various ways even by those who call themselves Christians. They are, however, the substance of what most Christian people believe about him and about his significance for themselves and for the world. Those who do believe in him in such a way are claiming that faith in Jesus is not just a set of religious convictions, nor just a sense of personal and individual salvation, nor just a code of moral laws. Christian faith may be all of those, but it is much more: faith in Jesus Christ claims to say something of cosmic importance about God, his creation, and all human beings.

There are, of course, easier ways of talking about Jesus and his significance for us today. Examples of such easier ways can be found from the very beginning of Christianity. In earlier centuries some of those ways usually (although not always, as we can see in the New Testament itself) emphasized his divine nature at the expense of his humanity. They talked about Jesus as though he were simply a god come to earth, taking on the visible appearance of a human being but not sharing our humanity and history in any serious way. Gnosticism, as that tendency is called, was one of the major sources of conflict in the early Church, and it was certainly the most serious challenge with which the Church was then faced — and even perhaps is today. The subject is a very complex one, but in essence gnosticism represented that attitude towards religion which can be characterized as a flight away from the concrete realities of time and space and of the history of human pain and suffering into a purely spiritual realm, an ethereal realm, indeed, from which vantage point flesh and blood could be regarded as something insignificant and even evil in itself. As we shall see later, it was to a considerable degree the struggle with gnosticism and its claim to offer a secret tradition of teaching that led to the development of an institutional ministry in the first centuries of the Church's history.

Gnosticism had consequences for the way in which some people talked about Jesus himself; it manifested itself in the early heresy known as docetism. As an attempt to define who and what Jesus was, docetism reflected the gnostic desire to remove him completely from the materiality of human existence and to consider him only a supernatural and god-like figure. In one form of gnosticism the divine Christ is pictured as watching the crucifixion from a distant hill and laughing to himself because he has deceived those who think they are killing him, when in fact they are only crucifying a shell of flesh: the real Christ is elsewhere. The problem for a docetic christology, as indeed for all forms of gnosticism, is that it cannot conceive of the eternal God involved in or really united to the messiness of human life. Religion is a flight from the world, and salvation is possible only for those few who can become pure spirits. Today it would be difficult to find a consistently developed docetic christology; the reason, I believe, is that we in a techno-logical and scientific culture find it much easier to talk about the human and fleshly reality of Jesus than to envisage him as purely spiritual and supernatural. That too can have its unfortunate consequences, for it can limit us to a very shallow view of reality. At least, however, it means that we do have to deal with the humanity of Christ and with our own humanity in anything we may say about him.

Unfortunately, however, gnosticism, of which docetism was a form of christological heresy, has not completely disappeared from Christianity, even though it may not be explicitly acknowledged for what it is. Contemporary forms of gnosticism may be reluctant to speak about Jesus in explicitly docetic terms, but the attitude towards him which docetism represented still runs as an undercurrent in the way many people think about themselves and the Church. Some Christians today, in the face of the terribly complex and shattering problems which threaten all human beings, would argue that the Christian Church should remain aloof from social and political concerns and should, rather, direct the attention and the energy of Christian people only to spiritual matters and to their eternal salvation. They would denounce the involvement of the Church in the political and economic order as a 'politicization' of the Gospel. Such a contemporary form of gnosticism, and of the docetic christology which it reflects, can be found, I believe, in the recent series of lectures by Dr Edward Norman, *Christianity and the World Order*.[1] Dr Norman says many things of interest about the various political situations in which Christians find themselves today, but the thrust of his argument is that the Church ought not to concern itself with such matters and that when it does (as in Latin America and South Africa) it is abandoning its true faith and calling as a spiritual community removed from the history of human suffering.

There are many criticisms which could be made of Dr Norman's thesis.[2] I am concerned here, however, only with what it implies about Jesus Christ. Dr Norman speaks of the Incarnation as the coming of Christ into the world, but that coming is described somewhat oddly from the point of view of traditional Christian faith. He writes: 'At the centre of the Christian religion, Christ remains unchanging in a world of perpetual social change and mutating values. To identify him with the passing enthusiasms of men — each one of which, in its time of acceptance, seems permanently true — is to lose him amidst the shifting superstructure of human idealism.' He then goes on to say that the coming of Christ into the world is the event in which 'the visible and the unseen world were briefly joined, and the supervening

6

force of the divine flowed down upon the earth'.[3] It would appear that for Dr Norman, Christ is a divine and spiritual figure, a fleeting presence among us, who is essentially aloof from our enthusiasms and, one would imagine, from our suffering and sin. He cannot be identified with us, but is only a visitor from another realm. That may be an easier way of talking about Jesus, but it is unfaithful to the New Testament as well as to the long history of Christian reflection upon the person and work of Jesus Christ. As I hope to show, the doctrine of the Incarnation has in various ways attempted to give expression to the Christian belief that in the life of a historical man, Jesus of Nazareth, something of universal importance is being said to us about our hopes and fears precisely because we believe that in his life God himself has come to share our lives and to identify himself with our flesh and blood. To believe that about Jesus is to believe also that the Church is not a society of especially holy and spiritual people who are concerned only with the ethereal matters of the spirit, but that it is an extension into daily life of the presence of the eternal God in human suffering and pain, a society which in its service to all human beings seeks to offer the sin and anguish of human history to the God who has become one with us and who brings us into union with himself in the life of Jesus of Nazareth. Christ is lost to us not when we identify him with our need, but when we do not believe in him as one who shares our need in the life of his Church.

Partly in reaction to the excessively supernatural and dogmatic view of Jesus, there has grown up since the last century an approach which is at the other end of the christological spectrum – a concern among theologians to re-establish Jesus as a human figure whose words and work express his life as a prophet and teacher of Judaism in the first century. This way of talking about Jesus, while having its roots in the early history of the Christian faith, reflects a change in the cultural climate of western Christianity in the past two hundred years, namely, a more empirical and scientific approach to the study of religion. Along with that change has also developed a recognition of the responsibility

7

of Christians to investigate critically and historically the origins of Christian belief and ecclesiastical institutions. For the very reason that Christianity claims to be rooted in historical events and not to be gnostic speculation, it must deal honestly with historical data. As we shall see in chapters 3 and 4 such studies have had very important consequences for our contemporary understanding of the ministry of the Church, and also for the way in which we understand Jesus and how we are to talk about him.

To a considerable degree that new approach to the study of Christian history has been very valuable indeed. It has enabled us to regain many of the images and themes in the New Testament story of Jesus which had been obscured for several centuries and to have a renewed appreciation of the significance of Jesus for us today. It has also enabled us to see more clearly how the Holy Spirit has guided the Church in the course of its history in the world. As with all new things, however, there have been some consequences which have required us to ask very serious and even disturbing questions about our faith in Jesus Christ. Some of the answers to those questions appear to be easier than those which Christians have been accustomed to give. However, as with docetism in its ancient and modern forms, the easier ways of talking about Jesus do not always take into account the witness of Holy Scripture, the theological tradition of the Church and, perhaps most important of all, the experience among Christian people in diverse times and places of the reality of Jesus Christ in their lives. They have, rather, given an easy answer to the hard question posed by the historical life of Jesus and by the continuing belief of Christian people that he is their saviour and lord. Jesus is a figure in history, and because he is we must do all that we can to understand him in terms of his historical reality. But he is also a figure in the experience of those who believe in him, because he continues to lay upon them a transcendent claim and call to holiness in the life of the Church. Both dimensions of who Jesus is are part of the data for our attempts to understand him, or, if not to understand *him*, to understand why it is we believe in him. Just as our new awareness of the importance of his history ought not to allow us to reduce his significance to abstract statements, so also our experience of him as saviour and lord ought not to allow us to reduce his significance to what can be justified by a contemporary form of empirical and positivistic philosophy.

One of the attempts to deal with some of the new questions put to us by the study of the historical origins of Christian faith can be found in a collection of essays which has caused some stir and debate, at least in Britain: *The Myth of God Incarnate*.[4] It is by no means definitive of the kind of christology which is being done by contemporary theologians in Europe and North America, nor does it reflect some of the concerns about traditional christology which are being raised by theologians in Latin America and Africa. It does, however, put the problem in fairly sharp focus. The problem with which the 'mythologists', as they have called themselves, were concerned, and around which the subsequent debate has centred, is how are we in the twentieth century, with our cultural prejudgements and presuppositions, to understand the significance of Christ for us today? Their basic contention is that the historical investigation of Christian origins leads us to say that the traditional doctrines about Christ as the incarnate Son of God and second Person of the Trinity are mythical and poetic ways of talking which may be untrue, and which certainly cannot speak to us in an empirical and scientific age. Therefore, a new way of talking about Jesus Christ and his significance for us needs to be developed. The essays, in various ways, attempt to examine the problem and to suggest some new ways of talking.

The criticisms of the book have been many, especially of its somewhat ambiguous and misleading use of the word 'myth'.[5] It is not my intention here to continue that debate, but rather to point to the general conclusion reached by the authors of the several essays (although it needs to be said that there are variations among them and different levels of theological sophistication) that what we say about Jesus Christ ought to be strictly confined to what is known through our historical investigation of the New Testament materials, and that his significance for us today must be stated in language which lays stress upon what we know of him from our historical investigations and not on the theological speculations of subsequent generations. What such a position requires, as the several authors of the essays recognize, is that we must learn to speak about Jesus Christ and his significance for us in ways which express only his reality as a human being living in a particular historical period. He can serve as an example to us in very profound ways and we can say that his life was one which shows to us not only how we are related to God but also how God sees us and regards us. But we cannot use about him language which identifies him in some unique way with the transcendent reality we call God.

On the other hand, many of the critics of *The Myth of God Incarnate* have argued that the traditional language used about Jesus, which does, in varying ways, identify him with God and name him the Son and Word, was a legitimate development in the Church's history in order to express what Christian people came to believe about him through prayer, sacrament, preaching, and the moral life. For the mythologists, Jesus the man is a *moral* example to us — moral perhaps in the most profound of senses, as Frances Young in her essay in that volume, 'A Cloud of Witnesses', makes clear — but his relationship to the Christian community now is across the gulf of history. For others, including myself, the significance of Jesus is to be found in his continuing presence to the Church; therefore who he is must be described in language which expresses his ultimate unity with the God whom he called Father and the Spirit whom he sends.

These two extreme points of view — the contemporary form of docetism and an exclusive emphasis upon the Jesus of history — express the problem which Christians have when speaking of Jesus. It is the problem, indeed it is the mystery, which has always been present for Christian belief because of the claims which Christians have made about him. He is not just a human being like us – but he is; he is not just God – but he is. Some people have called that way of talking the paradox of Christian belief about Jesus; others have called it the absurdity. St Paul called it a stumbling block and a folly; but, as he went on to say, 'to those who are called, both Jews and Greeks, Christ the power of God and the wisdom of God. For the foolishness of God is wiser than men, and the weakness of God is stronger than men' (1 Corinthians 1:22–5). In other words, when Christians speak of Jesus Christ we are speaking of a mystery to which our language can direct us but which it cannot totally disclose.

It was indeed, to deal with the mystery which Christ is that the bishops of the Church gathered at Chalcedon in 451. They sought to resolve a major crisis in the Church concerning the doctrine of Christ as the mystery of God's action in human history. The Council adopted a formal statement of the doctrine of the Incarnation by defining the kind of language which ought to be used about Christ. Because it is such an important statement historically in the development of Christian doctrine, yet not well known today by most people, I shall quote the Definition in full.

Therefore, following the holy fathers, we all with one accord teach men to acknowledge one and the same Son, our Lord Jesus Christ, at once complete in Godhead and complete in manhood, truly God and truly man, consisting also of a reasonable soul and body; of one substance (*homoousios*) with the Father as regards his Godhead, and at the same time of one substance with us as regards his manhood; like us in all respects, apart from sin; as regards his Godhead, begotten of the Father before the ages, but as yet regards his manhood begotten, for us men and for our salavation, of Mary the Virgin, the God-bearer (*Theotokos*); one and the same Christ, Son, Lord, Only-begotten, recognized in two natures, without confusion, without change, without division, without separation; the distinction of natures being in no way

11

annulled by the union, but rather the characteristics of each nature being preserved and coming together to form one person and subsistence, not as parted or separated into two persons, but one and the same Son and Only-begotten God the Word, Lord Jesus Christ; even as the prophets from earliest times spoke of him, and our Lord Jesus Christ himself taught us, and the Creed of the Fathers has handed down to us.[6]

The statement, in philosophical and theological language appropriate to the fifth century, has become a formal definition of how we are to speak of Jesus Christ. As a definition it needs much clarification, and to make the necessary clarifications and even modifications is part of the ongoing task of theology. But for many centuries it has been normative for the Church in describing the mystery of Christ, and it has become for many the foundation upon which the doctrine of the Church and the sacramental life could be built. I want here to say a few things about why I believe the Chalcedonian Definition is important, not only for christology in general, but also for its influence upon that movement and development in Anglicanism with which we are concerned.

Some things need to be said about the controversy which lay behind the Definition, although that need not detain us for long. Essentially, it involved finding the proper terminology for expressing the relationship between the human nature of Jesus and his divine nature as Son and Word of God, the second person of the Trinity. As the Church had reflected upon its faith in Jesus and as it had through its history experienced his saving presence in word and sacrament, Christian people had come to believe that in the historical man, Jesus of Nazareth, the eternal God was truly present and active. More than a hundred years earlier, at the Council of Nicea (from which the Nicene Creed is derived), St Athanasius had argued that in order for Christ to be our saviour it was necessary that he be truly of God, neither a demigod nor a creature, but truly of the same substance with the one whom he called Father. The word 'incarnation' expressed the conviction that God himself in the person of the Son and Word is truly present in a human life. He had become flesh, embodied, for us and for our salvation. Certainly, such a way of talking involves a great deal of what we might now call mythological language (that is, language which speaks about eternal things in a temporal way). The Fathers of Nicea, however, attempted to formulate what they believed about Jesus as saviour and lord by using the technical, philosophical term *homoousios*: of one substance or, as the modern translation of the Creed puts it, 'of one Being with the Father'.

By speaking in this way, the Fathers of Nicea had created a whole new set of problems, or rather new possibilities. In particular, they raised certain questions with which Christians had to deal: What do the terms humanity and divinity mean in such a context? How can we say that the eternal God is present and active in a human life? What kind of union beween two such natures is possible? The easiest way to answer such questions would have been simply to deny or at least minimize the humanity of Jesus or to make the union between humanity and divinity insignificant and trivial – much in the way some pagan mythologies speak of the gods coming to earth. This was the direction which some in the Church took. In what eventually became know as the Apollinarian heresy it was maintained that Jesus was truly a man only in the sense that he had a human, physical body. What we call the soul, that is, his reason and will, was in this case not a human soul but was the Son and Word of God, the second person of the Trinity. Incarnation was understood to mean that the Son of God was in the flesh of a human being, but that Jesus could not be thought of as a man in exactly the same sense as other human beings. On the other hand, in what eventually became known as the Nestorian heresy it was argued that Jesus was indeed truly a man, body and soul, but the language that was used about him made it very difficult to speak of a genuine, substantial *unity* between the Son of God and the man Jesus. Nestorianism had to argue for a unity which could not be personal or to use the technical

13

term, hypostatic. These two heretical movements, as they were declared to be, represented the extreme of two schools of thought which were reconciled (at least officially) in the Definition of Chalcedon. The school of Antioch, with which Nestorianism is associated, and the school of Alexandria, with which Apollinarianism is associated, were both struggling to say something of great importance about Jesus Christ and his saving work for us, but they had to find the language which expressed clearly and truthfully what they believed.

The Antiochenes were especially concerned to assert that Jesus is truly a human being, with all that humanity means: that he shares in our weakness, that he could have a sense of desolation (as his cry from the cross showed), and that his intellect and will are subject to the same limitations and freedom as those of any other human being. They argued that it is only in such a life that the Word and Son of God can be said to be present *for our salvation*. The Word dwells in the man Jesus without in any sense diminishing or negating his full human nature. The Alexandrians were quick to point out, however, that such a way of talking about the Incarnation made it difficult to assert the full and complete *unity* of God and Man. They accused the Antiochenes of presenting Jesus as a conjunction of natures, not a unity of humanity and divinity. And there is a certain truth to the accusation (although the position of the Antiochenes has been more fully developed by some theologians in our century). The language they used to describe what they believed did not speak clearly enough of the unity of God and Man, even though their concern to preserve the real, historical man, Jesus of Nazareth, is absolutely essential if we are to be faithful to the New Testament. The Antiochene position does not seem to present us, however, with a view of Christ which totallly and irrevocably commits the eternal God to human history.

The Alexandrians, most notably Cyril of Alexandria, attempted to deal with the mystery of Christ from another direction. While there is much that is controversial about

14

the theology of Cyril, he did, however, see something of great importance about Jesus Christ: that in him what we confess is the *personal* unity of God and Man. Some have argued that Cyril did not really accept the full humanity of Jesus, and there is much in his writings which would justify that point of view; but there is another way of interpreting him which, I believe, is not only correct but also more helpful in understanding what the Definition of Chalcedon was concerned to say. Cyril was seeking to find the language in which to say that the humanity of Jesus — that is, what it means for him to be a real human being and not a phantasm — finds its reality, its subsistence, its actuality, in the Word of God which takes human nature and makes it one with himself. This can be put another way — a way which has had deep significance for mystical theology in the East and West — by recalling a saying attributed to Athanasius: 'The Son of God became son of man so that the sons of men, that is, of Adam, might become sons of God . . . partakers of the life of God . . . . Thus He is Son of God by nature, and we by grace.'[7] In other words, what Cyril was pointing to, even though his terminology needed clarification, was that to be truly and genuinely human, to realize, as we might put it now, our human potential, we must become one with God in the humanity of the risen and exalted Christ — a position that, as we shall see, has figured prominently in much Anglican discussion about Jesus and his Church.

There is, of course, always the danger in this way of thinking and talking of losing sight of Christ's historical manhood in the worship and piety of Christian people. The basic insight, however, is fundamentally important for the doctrine of the Incarnation, both for what we understand about Jesus Christ and for what we understand about the Church and the sacramental life. It is pointing to the belief that men and women can find their true humanity only in God, only by sharing in the life of God through the humanity of Christ himself. The man Jesus is the true expression of our human nature through his union with the Son and Word of God, and we become truly human as we are incorporated by grace into his humanity. The realization

15

of our humanity, of our becoming the men and women we were created to be, is not something which we can achieve through our own moral effort or our own strengths. It is always God's gift: the gift of his Son to us in Jesus and the gift of grace poured into our hearts, making us children of God and heirs of eternal life. The Church then is the Body of Christ through which we are enabled to participate in the divine life.

The sometimes conflicting but also converging points of view of Antioch and Alexandria came to their final expression in the Definition of Chalcedon, and they have characterized the doctrine of the Incarnation ever since. The concepts and the philosophical context with which the Council had to work may be abstract and even foreign for us today, but the mystery of Christ which they seek to express is the mystery of the one who shows us the Father and who creates new life in us. I want to suggest three things of importance which the Definition says about our belief in him.

1 When it speaks of the divine nature in Christ, the definition is saying something of importance about the God in whom Christians believe. As we know from the study of other religious traditions, there are many ways in which humans have conceived of 'a supreme being'. Because of our roots in Judaism and because of Jesus Christ, who is, we believe, the full and definitive revelation of God, Christians have a quite definite concept of God. In the Old Testament God is one who is active and dynamic in the affairs of his people, making his will and purpose known in the lives of human beings, leading and directing them, saving and correcting them. The God of the Old Testament is not an isolated and aloof figure, nor is he a philosophical principle; he is rather the maker and restorer of all things. It is of this God, about whom the Jews learned in their history (and are learning still), that the Definition speaks when it says that in Jesus we must acknowledge one who is truly God the Word, 'even as the prophets from earliest times spoke of him, and our Lord Jesus Christ himself taught us, and the creed of the Fathers has handed down to

16

us'. In the human life of Jesus of Nazareth the eternal, triune God acts in the person of his Son and Word, and because of that definitive action in Jesus, he continues to be present, we believe, in the Church and in the history of all human beings through his Holy Spirit.

2 When it speaks of the human nature of Jesus Christ, the definition is saying something of importance about us – not only those who believe in him, but all human beings. Here, I believe, the insights of Antioch and Alexandria are significant. The school of Antioch saw very clearly that the human nature of Jesus could not be thought of simply as an abstraction, as something less than fully human. Jesus was a man. To forget that is not only to be untrue to the New Testament; it is also to forget something of vital importance in the mystery of our redemption, namely, that Jesus is our saviour and lord because he shares with us in all of the temptations, difficulties and pains which we know in our lives. That is the significance of the cross in Christian theology and devotion. On the cross, we believe, the suffering and sin of the world are offered to the Father in the death of him who is one with us and who shares our humanity with us.

But the insight of Cyril and the Alexandrians generally was not forgotten in the Definition. What it is to be a human being is not something which can be exhaustively and totally defined by our existence in time and space, and our human nature cannot be understood exclusively in terms of our individual histories and of what can be reported about us. There is more to being a man or a woman than we can grasp or define. Holy scripture and much of the theological tradition have called that 'something more' in human beings the spirit or the soul. Some contemporary philosophers have called it the dimension of transcendence, by which they mean that there is in every human life a mystery of love and freedom, an openness to God, which is a depth greater in us than we can fully comprehend. St Paul, in a profoundly mystical way, spoke of that dimension of depth in our humanity when he wrote to the Christians at Corinth: 'For now we see in a mirror

17

dimly, but then face to face. Now I know in part; then I shall understand fully, even as I have been fully understood' (I Corinthians 13:12). In God we shall know as we are known: that is our calling into the divine life. In Jesus, we believe, that full and total knowing and being known is his by nature; it is his oneness with the Son and Word of God. For us it is the gift of grace, the indwelling of the Spirit of Christ, and through that gift we grow into 'the unity of the faith and of the knowledge of the Son of God, to mature manhood, to the measure of the stature of the fullness of Christ' (Ephesians 4:13). The Incarnation says of our human nature that in Christ men and women are called into the fullness of life with God in order that they may be fully human.

3 That brings us to the final consideration: the nature of unity. The Definition defines the unity between God and man in Jesus as a *personal* unity. Certainly, the word person means something quite different for us today from what it did for the Fathers of the Council. There has been a rich development in the notion of person, personal and personality since the fifth century. I believe we can say, however, that what the Council intended by the concept is not radically dissimilar to what we mean when we use the word personal. When we now speak of a person or of personal unity, what we are trying to express is that sense of self-identity which makes it possible for us to know what we mean when we say 'I', even though we may not be able to define what we mean too precisely. What we are expressing is a sense of unity of purpose, which enables us to act, and to take responsibility for what we say and do. To be a person is to be one who is conscious of self, not so radically split apart into conflicting desires that we cannot act at all — a condition which would be described as pathological. And yet at the same time most people, indeed I suspect all people on reflection, would recognise themselves in St Paul's description of himself: 'I do not understand my own actions. For I do not do what I want, but I do the very thing I hate' (Romans 7:15). In spite of the disunity in ourselves we still have enough sense of our personal identity and unity to be

able to look forward to a deeper sense of personal unity – to that day when we shall know ourselves as we are known.

Such a way of thinking about personal unity as we experience it can help us to catch a glimpse of what the Definition is talking about when it speaks of Jesus Christ as the personal unity of God and man. What we, even in our disarray, anticipate in hope, Jesus is now. His heart, mind and will are one with the eternal Word and Son of God. To be God is not the same thing as to be man, and to be man is not the same thing as to be God; but in Jesus Christ God and man are united to one another in such a way that we can only say (stretching language to its limits) that they are one person, that in Jesus God the Son and Word has committed himself irrevocably and absolutely to our history and humanity. St John's gospel first expressed the confession of faith which Chalcedon was later to define: 'The Word became flesh and dwelt among us, full of grace and truth; we have beheld his glory, glory as of the only Son from the Father (John 1:14).

The Chalcedonian Definition is, thus, a foundation upon which we can build. Certainly it is not the only way of telling the story of Jesus and his saving work in the lives of Christian people, but it has been and continues to be one of the more significant ways through which we can catch a glimpse of who Jesus Christ is and how belief in him affects our understanding of ourselves and of the Church.

As I have said, the way in which we think and speak doctrinally about Jesus Christ has consequences for the way in which we understand and speak about the Church and the Christian life. (Of course, it is also true that the way in which we experience the reality of Christ in the Church and the sacramental life affects the way in which we think and speak about him doctrinally. I am concerned here, however, more with doctrinal expression than with our experience of him as saviour and lord, although the two cannot be separated.) The way of thinking and speaking about Jesus and the Church to which the Chalcedonian Definition led can be called an incarnational theology. It is a theology of the Church and of

19

the sacramental life which reflects upon how the doctrine of the Incarnation affects the prayer, worship and action of Christians in every area. It seeks to answer the question: If we believe in Jesus as incarnate lord, what are the consequences for the way in which we understand the Church, the sacraments and the moral life?

To show how such an incarnational theology has developed in the theological tradition would require a separate series of studies, for it is a point of view which has most often characterized the theology of the Orthodox Churches of the East as well as the Church in the West prior to the Reformation. Indeed, to a considerable degree (although with periods of serious decline and darkness) it could be said to be representative of the 'catholic tradition' in western theology. Some of the controversies at the time of the Reformation, which so decisively affected the Church of England, represented an explicit rejection of an incarnational approach to the Church and sacraments for reasons which were, as we can now see, perfectly valid. An incarnational theology, like all theological constructs, needs the corrective of other points of view; and it was this which, among other things, the Reformation accomplished. As I shall discuss in chapters 4 and 5, all theological points of view are constructs of human beings, and thus any particular theology needs the balance that other ways of understanding the Gospel can give. There are different ways of telling the story of Jesus, just as there are different ways of experiencing his saving work in our lives. Genuine ecumenism in the Church will always require a recognition of different theological perspectives; and indeed Anglicanism itself, as it has developed over the centuries, can be said to represent a search for unity in the midst of diversity. But this is a matter to which we shall return.

In Anglicanism, however, there has been a continuing tradition of an incarnational theology. It has appeared at various periods, been lost and then regained. At times it has been expressed primarily in ritualistic movements or in social action; at other times it has been a more academic and theological concern. But it has always involved a particular way of understanding the nature of the Church — a way that can be called 'catholic' if one does not define that difficult term in too narrow a way. Until the time of the Oxford Movement, the great representatives of an incarnational theology were to be found in the period immediately following the separation between Rome and Canterbury, when the Church of England was attempting to find its identity among the conflicting claims of the Reformed Churches on the Continent, the Puritans at home, and the Church of Rome. It was a tradition which was lost to a considerable degree in the eighteenth century, then regained in the nineteenth, to continue into our own time as one of the most characteristic and creative theological traditions in the Anglican Communion. That such a tradition had existed was important for the Oxford Movement itself, because it enabled Pusey, Newman and Keble to argue in the Tracts for the Times that they were in fact returning to or regaining an authentic Anglican doctrine of the Church and not advocating a Romish innovation.

What that incarnational approach represented in Anglicanism can be indicated through a brief examination of the thought of its greatest exponent, Richard Hooker (1554–1600). He was a principal spokesman for the Church of England during one of its most turbulent periods. Not only was he a major theologian in his own right (it is said that even the Pope admired his work), but he was the first Anglican apologist who quite consciously placed the doctrine of the Incarnation as expressed in the Chalcedonian Definition at the centre of his theology, and on that basis argued against those who accused the Church of England either of abandoning the authority of scripture or of rejecting ancient Catholic tradition. His major work, *The Laws of Ecclesiastical Polity*, influenced many who came after him, most especially the theologians, preachers and apologists of the Church of England in the next generation who are known as the Caroline divines. Although not all of the leaders of the Oxford Movement agreed with him on every point (Newman, for example, did not agree with his views on human reason), it is not insignificant that the first critical edition of the *Laws*, and what was until recently the standard text of that great work, was edited by John Keble in 1836, at the height of the Oxford Movement.

Hooker's chief contribution to the development of an incarnational tradition within Anglican theology is to be found in two areas. The first is his discussion of the nature of law and his attempt to ground the positive laws and customs of the Church of England in a theology which centred upon the rational and providential ordering of creation in the eternal law of God. The second is his discussion of the sacramental nature of the Church and its relationship to the Incarnation. It is in the second area that he provided a foundation upon which others were to build, but in both the doctrine of the Incarnation is central, albeit in different ways. The Chalcedonian Definition expressed for him the truth about the order of creation as well as the truth about the order of grace in the Church.

The Reformation was a period of radical change in the western Church and of often violent theological controversy. It produced many polemical writings and harsh criticisms of the teaching and practice of the Roman Church as the Reformers sought to restore the Church of Christ to what they believed was its primitive purity in belief and practice. Underneath all of the controversies there was one fundamental theological doctrine which, whatever their differences in other ways, united the Reformers; around it all other issues revolved. That doctrine was justification by grace through faith, namely, that no human institution and no human being can stand between the believer and the absolute demand of God; the only mediator between God and man is Jesus Christ, in whom we are accounted as righteous before God. Certainly all Christians ought to accept and believe the doctrine of justification as it was developed in the theology of St Paul, for it is basic to the understanding of our redemption through God's free gift of himself to us sinners. However, as is also true of the doctrine of the Incarnation, how a doctrinal formulation is worked out in the life of the Church can make a great deal of difference to the way in which it is understood and to the way it affects other aspects of the Christian life. For the Reformers, struggling as they were against what they saw as the corruptions of the Church and the sacramental system, the doctrine of justification enabled them to cut away accretions and return to the message of the Gospel: man in his sinfulness can lay no claim upon God, either from his reason or from his good works. The only foundation is the faithfulness of Christ and his free gift of grace, which breaks down and shatters all human presumption.

From such a radical way of understanding the doctrine of justification there arose as well the doctrine of predestination and the distinction between the visible and invisible Church. For the Reformers the Church, as a visible and structured community in history, was important but it could not assure salvation; therefore this visible and institutional Church with its sacramental system and its rites and ceremonies no longer occupied the place of pre-eminent authority and power in the scheme of salvation which earlier in Christian history it was believed to have. Those whom God had elected and predestined to salvation formed the invisible Church of the redeemed – the Church known only to God and not to be identified with the visible and institutional Church in the world. In the heart of the Reformation controversies, such a view could only be seen as in radical opposition to the Catholic doctrine of the Church and sacraments.

Hooker, however, even though he was affected by the teaching of the Reformers, looked back to an older patristic and medieval view, and established in the emerging self-consciousness of the Church of England an incarnational theology which attempted to understand the order of creation and the order of grace in quite different terms.

For Hooker the order of creation, (that is, everything that exists save God himself – the natural order, as we call it) is governed by reason and law. Because it is governed by reason and law, it can be understood rationally by human beings who can know the law of nature and who can be expected to follow it even though they may not be believers in what God has made known of himself in Christ. Human

23

reason as such participates in the rationality of God as human law participates in the eternal law of God. What such a view of the order of creation meant in Hooker's theology was that the divine-human relationship, which was to find its fullest expression in the Incarnation, has its foundation in the very being of God. In Jesus Christ God reveals himself as one whose nature is to be in relation to his creation; his taking of our humanity in the Incarnation is the ultimate and most personal expression of his eternal self-giving and care for that which he has brought into being. For Hooker, God is always working through the things of the world, through human history in all of its chances and changes, in order to make known his purpose and to bring that purpose about. Law is the rational expression of that ordering, and through it we can see that the created order, human history and human nature itself have a participation in the divine ordering of all things even while they continue to be what they are — temporal, finite and created. The doctrine of the Incarnation, as expressed in the Chalcedonian Definition, is thus true not only in what it says about the person and natures of Jesus Christ; it is also true in what it says about the structure of all created being. All created things are related to God in their very nature; God is present to them in varying degrees without destroying or negating their created existence; and they participate in his being through his willing presence to them. The Incarnation of God in Christ is God's *personal* presence to the created order. It is the ultimate expression in our humanity of who God is: personal being. The belief that God is personal being is the substance of the doctrine of the Trinity, namely, that God is Father, Son, and Holy Spirit.

In such a context as this — vastly different from the context of the Reformers — Hooker discusses the significance of the doctrine of the Incarnation for the Church and the sacramental life. In Book V of the *Laws* he develops an incarnational theology in explicit terms: as the order of creation is related to God through law, so the Church is the community of persons related to God through grace. He sums up his incarnational theology of the Church and sacraments in a masterful way:

> Thus therefore we see how the Father is in the Son and the Son in the Father; how They both are in all things, and all things in Them; what communion Christ hath with his Church, and His Church and every member thereof is in Him by original derivation, and He personally in Them by way of mystical association wrought through the gift of the Holy Ghost, which They that are His receive from Him, and together with the same what benefit soever the vital force of His Body and Blood may yield, yea by steps and degrees They receive the complete measure of all such divine grace, as doth sanctify and save throughout, till the day of their final exaltation to a state of fellowship in glory, with Him whose partakers they are now in those things that tend to glory.[8]

There is nothing here which will not be developed and deepened by the Oxford Movement and later by those who have inherited that tradition. There are, however, two matters of particular importance in the passage to which I want to call attention because they show the contrast to the Reformation tradition against which the leaders of the Oxford Movement saw themselves as struggling.

The first is that for Hooker the Church as a visible society in the world has its being, its ground of existence, in who Jesus Christ is. Its origin is in no sense accidental nor is it a human creation. The Church shares in the reality of Christ, the Incarnate One, as he shares in the reality of God. To be a member of the Church is to be incorporated into the humanity of Christ and so to participate in the divine life of the Son and Word. Just as the whole natural order is related to God by law, so the Incarnation is that event which expresses the relationship of human beings to God. In Christ human beings are called to share in the divine life; to bring that calling into its fullness is the purpose and reason for being of the Church.

In the second place, the way to that glory, as Hooker calls it, is the sacramental life of the Church. Through the sacraments, most especially baptism and eucharist, we are incorporated into Christ and we receive the grace which sanctifies us and gives to us the hope of eternal glory. In other words, through the sacraments we are partakers with Christ, we share in his life, we are mystically united to him even as we look to our final exaltation in him. As God gives himself in Christ, so Christ gives himself in his Church so that by grace we may grow into him. The grace of Christ in his Church enables us to become truly ourselves, to participate in the fullness of his humanity and to attain to the fullness of Christ in the life of the Holy Trinity.

Incarnation, Church and Sacraments: that is the Catholic theology to which Hooker first gave expression in the Church of England. Later generations, following in that tradition, will speak of the Church as having a divine commission, as being the extension of the Incarnation, and as being the sacrament of Christ. All of that development would raise many questions and problems for Anglicanism as it struggled to find its own identity as a community within the Catholic Church. It would also enable Anglicanism to discover a gift in its own heritage which it may yet be privileged to give to other communities within the Catholic Church.

2 The Oxford Movement: a Vision Regained

In chapter 1 I suggested one possible way to understand the relationship between the doctrine of Christ as incarnate lord and the doctrine of the Church as a sacramental and incarnational community. That particular vision, articulated first by Hooker, continued in the Church of England for some generations, during the seventeenth century in the works of the Caroline divines and then during the eighteenth in more obscure ways, through the bishops of the Scottish Episcopal Church and in isolated parishes in the country. Dr Pusey himself maintained that he had heard from his mother the basic principles for which the Oxford Movement stood when he was learning the Catechism. The Book of Common Prayer (1662) itself preserved something of that vision, even though it was strangely mixed with doctrinal positions that reflected Reformation controversies. Although the vision of the Church as an incarnational and sacramental community was not totally lost, it was certainly obscured in the eighteenth century, a period when the Church of England was dominated by latitudinarian politics and deistical philosophy.

Latitudinarianism emphasized the national character of the Church of England as the established Church. As a state Church it had to be broad enough to accommodate a wide spectrum of religious beliefs and practices, and its first obligation was seen to be the defence of the moral and political establishment of the nation. It was more or less a department of state, bound to the government by financial and political ties, without any independent authority of its own. Some students of the eighteenth century have pointed to the significance of the fact that in churches built in the eighteenth century, both in England and in the American colonies, the royal arms and the ten commandments were more prominently displayed than the altar. Architectural designs can say a great deal about the status of the Church in a society!

An equally important factor in the eighteenth century, which contributed greatly to the spiritual decline of the Church in England as well as in the colonies, was a philosophical outlook characterized as deism and its corollary scepticism. The eighteenth century was a time when great advances were made in scientific knowledge and when the light of reason was held to be all-important, condemning what was seen as 'religious superstition'. Many traditional Christian beliefs about the nature of God and the meaning of revelation in holy scripture were viewed very sceptically. God was thought of as a rational law-giver, a cosmic principle necessary perhaps to explain the cosmic order. The sense, however, that he was a living and acting presence in history was dismissed as a holdover from the childish history of the human race. In other words, it was a philosophical point of view which made the doctrine of the Incarnation, as I have discussed it in the preceding chapter, of little significance. Jesus could be thought of as a great teacher of moral and spiritual truths, and the Church which he had founded could still be highly regarded for its moral and spiritual influence in society, but any suggestion that the Church might be the sacramental presence of God in history and a community with a divine foundation and commission was rarely taken with great seriousness.

Most students of the eighteenth century would agree that, not only in England but in most parts of the Christian world, this was a time of aridity for the Church. There were, of course, reactions to that aridity. In England the Wesleyan movement and in America the Great Awakening called for spiritual renewal at all levels of society, and many were swept up by enthusiasm and believed in a new outpouring of the Spirit. Those movements, however, had little effect upon the established Church in England or upon the Episcopal Church in America. In both Churches what was not latitudinarian could best be described, as it was in America, as 'high and dry' – the identification of the Church with the Tory party in Great Britain and with the wealthy in the United States.

The first few decades of the nineteenth century saw the beginning of those two movements which were so drastically to change the Church of England and to have consequences for Anglicanism in other parts of the world: the Oxford Movement and the Evangelical revival. It is unfortunately beyond the scope of this book to consider the Evangelical party in the Church of England or its counterpart in the United States, but its importance was and has continued to be great. Several of the influential figures in the Oxford Movement came from Evangelical families and continued to share in some aspects of the Evangelical tradition. The leaders of both the Oxford Movement and of the Evangelical party correctly identified the real enemy to the Church, although they attempted to combat that enemy in different ways. The enemy was dryness, aridity, and indifference in the spiritual life; theologically it was a loss of a sense of God as one who calls and sanctifies human beings through Christ and the Spirit and who has revealed himself and his will in scripture and in the life of the Church.

For the Evangelicals the way to combat that enemy was through personal conversion, holiness of life, and a Spirit-filled piety, all of which were exemplified in the lives of those who formed what was known as the Clapham Sect, a group in which the Wilberforce family was most prominent. The Evangelical movement, however, was little concerned with the institutional and sacramental life of the Church and was much more concerned with the individual who is touched by God and converted to a new life. For the leaders of the Oxford Movement, on the other hand, the common enemy was to be combated first and foremost by regaining a true vision of the Church – not just the Church of England, nor just the Anglican Communion, but that body existing in all times and places, the One, Holy, Catholic and Apostolic Church of which the creeds and the Fathers spoke.

My concern here is with the vision of the Church which developed out of that complex and controversial period, and how that vision transformed Anglicanism in its own time and regained a tradition of catholicism in Anglicanism which continues to this day. The vision grew and changed in the course of the century, and it was blurred and uncertain at times; but it was a vision which was drawn from the tradition of the Church in the Fathers, which centred in the Incarnation, and which called Anglicanism to a deeper sense of its place within the larger Christian community. That vision involved three matters of great importance which I want to consider: the Church as an incarnational, sacramental body; the Church as catholic and apostolic; and the Church as One in Christ.

One of the mistaken judgements commonly made of the Oxford Movement is that it was excessively concerned with the institutional structures of the Church and with the outward and visible signs of piety. Certainly this was a judgement made at the time. In novels and cartoons, the leaders of the Oxford Movement were sometimes ridiculed and often treated with mild disdain because of their religious practices. Those who have read the Barchester novels of Anthony Trollope will remember the amusement with which he tells of the unusual practices adopted by well-bred ladies and clergymen who had been influenced by the goings-on in Oxford. Archdeacon Grantly and his supporters, on the other hand, regarded themselves as 'high churchmen' because they defended the rights and privileges of the established Church and opposed certain 'low-church' ecclesiastics strenuously, but there is little sense that they regarded themselves as called and commissioned to be the ministers of God's sacramental grace in the Church. They were first of all gentlemen, and the Establishment of which they were a part was a comfortable body of people living respectable and even religious lives, but not a Church known for proclaiming the incarnational and sacramental mystery at the heart of the Christian life.

The Oxford Movement, by contrast, called on people to

look more deeply into the institutional life of the established Church to discover its inner mystery as the Body of Christ. In reading the Tracts one discovers beneath the concern for institutional structures a deep piety and spirituality, and even more a sense that the Tractarians' concern about institutions and their outward forms arose from what they believed about Jesus Christ as Lord of the Church. The immediate situation called for a defence of the Church against those who would, as they thought, destroy it. As the Movement gathered strength they were more and more nourished by a sacramental spirituality and devotion which had much wider implications.

The immediate issue was state control and the usurpation by the government of the authority which belonged to the Church, especially to its bishops as successors to the apostles. But the issue was deeper than that, for the question which the Tractarians faced was the nature of the Church itself and its divine foundation and commission; they thus turned to that other vision of the Church which I have called sacramental and incarnational, for such a vision must be the basis of any doctrine about the authority of the Church which is not simply magical or archaeological.

It was evident to anyone reading the Book of Common Prayer that the Church of England had preserved a sacramental system at the centre of its life of worship. The Thirty-nine Articles, to which all clergy in the nineteenth century had to subscribe, also spoke of the importance of the sacraments, while attempting to purge them of Romish corruptions. But a sacramental system can be regarded in different ways. The sacraments of baptism and eucharist can be seen more or less as ordinances, carried out because they were commanded by Jesus, and important because they recalled to mind the founder of the Church, but of little significance to Christian life. In such a way of thinking, they may be important appendages but they are not integral to the Church's very nature. As we have seen, Hooker developed another point of view. Following the Fathers and, as he believed, the New Testament itself, the sacramental system expressed the very nature of the Church

31

and united the faithful through grace to the incarnate Christ himself. The Church is sacramental not simply because it was founded by Jesus but because it is his graceful presence in the lives of human beings.

It was this vision of the Church which became so central to the Oxford Movement, first as it was expressed in the Tracts and later in sermons, manuals of devotion and theological treatises. The Church was seen as the community of grace, the means through which we share in the life of God in Christ, and as the present embodiment of Christ himself by his Spirit in the world. Therefore, it could be nothing less than sacramental: the visible presence of the invisible God; his redeeming act towards his people in their history, working through people, institutional structures, and the things of creation — water and bread and wine. Nowhere, perhaps, is such view better expressed than in Dr Pusey's Tract on baptism (Tract 67) and in his several writings on the eucharist (Tract 81 and his sermon 'The Holy Eucharist a Comfort to the Penitent'). In those writings Pusey draws upon the scriptures, the writings of the Fathers (especially Cyril of Alexandria) and a host of earlier Anglican divines, to show that in those two sacramental acts of the Church our redemption in Christ is made real and present to us through God's use of the things of creation, and that through them we are truly incorporated into and participate in the real humanity of Christ himself. In the sacraments a new principle of life is imparted to us as we are united to Christ in the Church.

Such a way of seeing the Church and the sacraments would lead others in the Oxford Movement to speak in even stronger language of our mystical participation in Christ through the sacraments. The sacramental system of the Church is seen as the presence now of the incarnate Christ, not only a means of grace, but even more the present expression and action of God in Christ. As one of the writers of the period could say: '[Christ] is (what an awful thought!) *continually* incarnate in his Church.'[1] The Incarnation, the Church and the sacramental life are one continuous thread, joined to one another as the complete expression of how God works in the world, how he is continuously present to it and in it as he is present in Christ himself. As Robert Wilberforce in his great treatise on the Incarnation could say, the Church is in the world as Christ, the hypostatic union of God and Man, a divine and human society through which we are made partakers of Christ and so share in the life of the triune God.[2]

Such a high view of the sacramental and incarnational nature of the Church had consequences in many directions. It led, certainly, to a deep sacramental piety which has characterized the catholic movement in Anglicanism − a piety which today is, perhaps, one of the most important gifts we have to give to other Christian churches. It led also to the ritualist movement later in the century when priests of the Church in England and elsewhere sought to express the mystery of the Church in rich ceremonial.[3] And it led as well to the involvement of the Church in apostolic work with the poor and oppressed. It led finally to a deepening sense of the catholicity and apostolicity of the Church itself and to that fervent hope for unity which has so characterized Anglicanism in this century.

Correlative with the deepening sense of the Church as the sacramental presence of the incarnate Christ in the world was the increasing concern of the Oxford Movement with the meaning of catholicity and apostolicity, especially as these found expression in Anglicanism. The claim of the Church of England to be continuous with the ancient Church of the creeds even after the separation from Rome was not new to Anglican thought. That understanding of the Church had been put forward and vigorously defended by Hooker at the time of the Reformation controversies, and it had been preserved by others in the Caroline period and beyond. Those divines had insisted that the Church of England was the true Catholic and Apostolic Church of the land, reformed from certain abuses and refusing to acknowledge the claims of Rome, but not to be identified with movements which they considered sectarian and novel. Once again, however, the significance of those claims had been obscured in the eighteenth century. The established Church might have nothing to do with Dissenters, but in its official life the consequences of apostolicity and catholicity were scarcely recognized. Any such recognition would have raised the old fears of popery, as indeed happened when the Tracts began to appear in the next century.

From the very first the writers of the Tracts sought to reclaim for their own time the catholic and apostolic heritage of the Church of England and to show the consequences of a belief in that heritage for the life of the Church and its ministry. The meaning, or rather the meanings, of the terms 'catholicity' and 'apostolicity' are elusive. Unless one is willing to define them, as some have been willing to do, exclusively in terms of communion with the Roman See, they can mean very different things to different church traditions. And they meant different things to many in the Oxford Movement. Many of the Tractarians struggled (there is no better word to describe the process) with their meaning for the Church of England. From that struggle there emerged two considerations of the first importance, namely, that they were to be defined in terms of purity of doctrine and of apostolic succession in the episcopate.

The notion of purity of doctrine had many sides to it in the Oxford Movement, but through all of the controversies there was one underlying concern. It was a concern which Newman eventually saw to be unsatisfactory and which led him to Rome. But it was a concern which also led before the end of the nineteenth century to the liberal catholicism of Charles Gore and the *Lux Mundi* group, which is discussed in chapter 3. Pusey best represents it, and he defended it exhaustively in all of his writings. This concern was that the Church of the Fathers, the undivided Church of the first centuries of Christianity, taught and held the true catholic and apostolic faith in its purest form, and that any church at the present time which claimed to be Catholic must look back to the Fathers and accept their common teaching. Pusey found ample support for such a position in Anglican formularies and in the writings of the Caroline divines, and because he found support there he could uphold such a position as the genuine tradition of Anglicanism. His position on the purity of the Catholic faith in the period of the Fathers led, among other things, to the publication of the *Library of the Fathers* and the *Library of Anglo-Catholic Theology*, and for that reason alone it could be commended, since both were monumental works of scholarship. But from a theological point of view it was a difficult position to maintain with any consistency. And, because it could not allow for growth and development in the Church's understanding of itself and its place in the world, it resulted in a somewhat static view of catholicity. Newman, on the other hand, saw that there must be a more dynamic sense of the Church and a recognition that doctrine does develop in the history of the Church, bringing out new dimensions of the truth contained in Holy Scripture. As we shall see in chapter 3, Newman's position became accepted in the next century in both Anglicanism and Roman Catholicism, although it took the Church of Rome, to which Newman's stance led him, somewhat longer. But the appeal to antiquity as the true test of catholicity provided Pusey and others in the Oxford Movement with strong arguments against papal claims and sectarian innovations, and it restored to the Church of England an awareness of the vital importance of its continuity with the past and a sense of tradition, in contrast to a shallow modernism which would dismiss the past as irrelevant and antiquarian. As such the appeal to antiquity has remained a serious concern in every subsequent catholic interpretation of Anglicanism.

An even more important consideration, however, because it became a major symbol — even preoccupation — of the Oxford Movement, was the emphasis placed upon apostolic succession in the episcopate. Probably more has been written and argued about this contribution of the Tractarians than any other. Apostolic succession has been called the 'shibboleth of Anglo-Catholicism', but it has also come to be seen as the great gift which Anglicanism can bring to non-episcopal churches of Christendom. The claim that the bishops of the Church of England stood in succession to the apostles by the laying on of hands was certainly not originated by the Tractarians. Tract 74, for example, was a compendium of witnesses drawn from earlier periods of the Church of England to the importance of apostolic succession (although it needs to be said that some of the divines cited would have been somewhat less rigid in their interpretation of its significance than were the Tractarians themselves). The claim, of course, has always been an important one — and is so still — because it enabled the Church of England to identify itself visibly, that is through continuing institutional structures, with the Catholic and Apostolic Church of the creeds, and thus to counter the claims of Rome and to develop a sense of national catholicism. It was especially important for the Tractarians because it gave them a firm base from which to object to control of the Church by the State. Indeed, as Cardinal Newman said at a later time, the doctrine of apostolic succession was initially put forward in the Tracts for political purposes when the government sought to abolish or to reform some of the ancient episcopal sees. The claim that bishops had a divine authority transmitted to them from Christ himself through the apostles countered the prevalent practice of regarding the bishops of the Church simply as government appointees. But, of course, the claim meant much more than that. I shall say more about the significance of apostolic succession for Anglicanism, in chapter 3; here I want only to point to several aspects of its importance for the Oxford Movement.

It is important first of all to recognize that whatever the doctrine came to represent at a later period, for the writers of the Tracts it was deeply grounded in their understanding of the Church as a sacramental body. In the Tracts which deal with the importance of apostolic succession the subject is in virtually every case related to the eucharistic celebration. The succession is seen as a way of guaranteeing or assuring that the eucharist being celebrated is in continuity with the last supper itself and that the faithful are truly receiving the Body and Blood of Christ at the hands of a commissioned priest. The notion of commission is what is important here, and it should not, I think, be confused with the later notion of validity. What concerned the writers of the Tracts was not that orders simply be 'valid', but that the apostolic ministry of the Church be centred in the eucharistic act, the two together constituting a communion with the Church of the apostles. That a minister is duly commissioned means that he acts not with his own authority only, but with the authority of Christ given to the apostles. For that reason the apostolic ministry of the Church, maintained through the succession of bishops, is itself sacramental: an earthly institutional structure through which, in spite of all the sins and failures of human beings, God chooses to be present to his people. Indeed, Newman in somewhat passionate language almost longs for the day when priests will no longer be respected because they are gentlemen but because they have been entrusted with 'the awful and mysterious gift of making the bread and wine Christ's Body and Blood' (Tract 10).

In the second place the doctrine of apostolic succession called forth on the part of the Tractarians a deeper reflection on the nature of the Church of England as a *via media* and so gave rise to a longing for unity. In the first series of Tracts, published in 1833–34, Newman put forward the idea of the Church of England as a *via media* between the Protestantism of the Reformers and the Church of Rome. While he later repudiated the idea and recanted his strong anti-romanism, the idea persisted that the Church of England, and Anglicanism as a whole, represented a reformed Catholicism, free from the errors of both Geneva and Rome and so holding forth a vision of a Catholic and Apostolic Church which could show forth in its ministry, doctrine and liturgy the truth of both the Reformation and Rome. The notion of Anglicanism as a *via media* will need a much richer development than it received from the Tractarians themselves, because for them, as we shall see, it meant that the Church of England ought to seek unity only with those churches which had retained apostolic succession. Furthermore, it did not lead the Tractarians themselves to a deeper appreciation of the theology of the

Reformers and to the truth of the Gospel which may have been exemplified in the Reformation. But that Anglicanism could show forth in its history a way between Rome and Geneva and thus in its continuing existence hold Catholicism and Protestantism in tension with one another would become in the future a unique gift to offer to other Christian communities. The concern for apostolic succession has meant that the Church of England, while being a small national Church and one certainly affected in many ways by the Reformation and its theological controversies, has always been forced to ask itself how it stands in relation to that One, Holy, Catholic and Apostolic Church which has existed in all times and places, which has communion with the apostles, and which is the continuing sacramental presence of Christ. This question faces not only the Church of England, but all Anglicans, and they have not always answered it in a very satisfactory way. To the degree that it has led them to unchurch other Christian communities, the charge that apostolic succession has become the 'shibboleth of Anglo-Catholicism' rings true. Some Anglicans, unable to answer it at all, have turned to the Roman Catholic Church and to the logical and precisely formulated doctrine of what it means to be catholic and apostolic which seems to characterize Roman Catholicism. Others, however, have seen that Anglicanism is called to a particular work in the universal Church of Christ for the very reason that it knows in its own history the tension between Catholicism and Protestantism and, therefore, can represent the hope of all Christians for unity. I believe the first steps taken towards unity by the Oxford Movement were mistaken, but they have nevertheless shown us another path to take.

The early Tracts were characterized by strong, often chauvinistic, anti-romanism, and throughout his life Dr Pusey felt compelled to defend himself against the charge of popery. But the desire that the Church of England should seek for unity with Rome and also with the Orthodox Churches in the East soon became a major concern of the Oxford Movement. Little attention was given to union with the Protestant Churches on the Continent (the attempt to establish a form of union with the Lutherans through the Jerusalem episcopate was rejected by most of the Tractarians) and even less to the Dissenters at home. Pusey in fact once wrote that the course of his life had been such that he had never had any occasion to meet a Dissenter! It was to Rome largely that the Oxford Movement looked. In this, as in so many other ways, Pusey, after the departure of Newman, became the great leader. In addition to many sermons and personal letters, he wrote three volumes, which he called *Eirenicons*, in the hope of bringing about a greater understanding and peace between the Church of Rome and the Church of England, although in each making clear what he objected to in Roman practice and teaching. It was, however, at the end of the century and after Pusey's death that the first significant attempts were made by those representing the Tractarian tradition towards reunion with Rome. In 1889 Lord Halifax, then president of the English Church Union, the organization which carried on the concerns of the Oxford Movement, met the Abbé Portal, and they together worked towards the establishment of a papal commission to investigate the question of Anglican orders. The sad outcome of that attempt was the papal Bull of 1896, 'Apostolicae Curae', which declared Anglican orders 'absolutely null and utterly void' and called for the submission of Anglicans to the See of Peter.

It is not my intention here to argue against the Bull — many Roman Catholic historians and theologians now regard it as based upon quite false historical and theological assumptions. But the controversy is significant because it shows the degree to which the historic episcopate and apostolic succession had become a major concern for Anglicanism; at the same time it created a hope for unity which would go far beyond the desire or need to prove (as Newman once said) that the Church of England was truly Catholic.

What moved Lord Halifax and the Abbé Portal was the hope that a recognition that the Church of England possessed the historic episcopate and therefore that its ministers exercise a valid sacramental ministry could lead to some form of corporate reunion with Rome. While both men themselves certainly had a deep sense of the catholicity and apostolicity of the Church, their attempt to base corporate reunion upon the unbroken succession of bishops in the Church of England and, therefore, exclusively upon the notion of the validity of orders hardened an unfortunate tendency in the Oxford Movement and in much subsequent Anglo-Catholicism. It turned the question of catholicity and apostolicity predominantly towards the past, towards, that is to say, a static and archaeological doctrine of the Church and the ministry. As we have seen, that tendency was always present in the Oxford Movement. When that tendency was hardened in reference to the ministry and to apostolic succession, it meant the isolation of the validity of orders from the broader concern for apostolic teaching and worship. Validity became for many Anglo-Catholics the *sine qua non* of the ministry and of sacramental ministrations. Thus there could, and indeed did, develop the peculiar idea that valid orders make a Church Catholic, rather than a recognition of the fundamental truth that orders are one aspect of the fullness of Catholicity, not a proof of it.

As we shall see such a view of the apostolic ministry has had unhappy consequences for Anglican relations with Rome and with the Churches of the Reformation, for it has sometimes obscured how apostolic succession in the episcopate ought to mean more than conferring valid orders upon other churches or than having Anglican orders recognized by the Roman Catholic Church. The historic episcopate ought, rather, to be seen as the sacramental sign of the Church's communion and continuity in every age with its past in doctrine, worship and mission; and it is, therefore, itself an incarnational reality in the Church's life, expressing how Christian people are called to live in unity with the one shepherd and bishop, the one high priest, Jesus Christ. It was the next generation of Anglo-Catholics who would explore the deeper theological significance of the relationship between the apostolic ministry and the historic episcopate.

3   The Anglican Church: Catholic and Apostolic

The Oxford Movement had its limitations, but its most significant contribution to the Church of England and to the growing Anglican Communion throughout the world was that it enabled the Church of England to begin to regain a vision of the Church as catholic and apostolic and to bring that vision to bear upon the life of the Church in every area: worship, the life of prayer and mission. It was to the divine commission of the Church that those who inherited the tradition of the Tractarians in the next generation devoted themselves. Anglo-Catholicism moved in two directions. One direction, which can only be touched on briefly here was a major force in the Church's life: the deepening of the spiritual and pastoral life of the Church through liturgical revival and renewal, sacramental spirituality and pastoral care. This aspect of the Oxford Movement at first manifested itself in the ritualistic controversies which so afflicted the Church of England and the Episcopal Church in the United States at the end of the nineteenth century, as parish priests sought to express the sacramental and incarnational nature of the Church in the lives of their people. As we can now see, ritualism in the Anglican Church, whatever unhappy forms it may at times have taken, rested upon serious theological convictions about the nature of the Church as an incarnational community. But the spiritual and pastoral concern of the Oxford Movement also manifested itself in a new sense of mission and ministry. It led to apostolic work by Anglo-Catholics in many parts of the world and to an increased sense of the Church's vocation to serve the poor and oppressed. That concern was never better expressed

41

than in the famous address by Frank Weston, Bishop of Zanzibar, to the Anglo-Catholic Congress of 1923. In his talk on 'Our Present Duty', he ended with the words which are still a call and challenge to all Anglicans:

> You have got your Mass, you have got your Altar, you have begun to get your Tabernacle. Now go out into the highways and hedges where not even the Bishops will try to hinder you. Go out and look for Jesus in the ragged, in the naked, in the oppressed and sweated, in those who have lost hope, in those who are struggling to make good. Look for Jesus. And when you see him, gird yourselves with his towel and try to wash their feet.

In the history of the Oxford Movement and of its successors, the ritualistic controversies should never be allowed to obscure the courageous work of missionaries, religious, parish priests and lay people to bring about a new sense of holiness in the Church's life.

The other direction was the need for more serious theological reflection on the fundamental questions raised by the Tractarians about the doctrine of the Church, its sacramental life, the ministry, and the authority of the Church in the world, so that some of those questions could be explored more deeply and the theological concerns of the Tractarians be broadened in response to many new challenges. In 1891 a group of young theologians at Oxford, under the editorship of Charles Gore, published a collection of essays on these themes, entitled *Lux Mundi: A Series of Studies in the Religion of the Incarnation*. It is one of the most significant turning points in the history of Anglican divinity as a whole, but in particular it transformed the heritage of the Oxford Movement by enabling those who would identify themselves as Anglo-Catholics to lead the Church in new directions in the next century. And it remains a significant dimension of the catholic tradition and heritage for Anglicanism as it faces another new century.

There are two ways in which the effects of *Lux Mundi*

are, I believe, of continuing significance, even though those who have inherited the authors' tradition may not agree with all that they said. First, *Lux Mundi* represented the victory of the Oxford Movement in Anglicanism as a whole. Second, it enabled Anglo-Catholics, however they might disagree on particular issues, to confront the modern world and its manifold problems and challenges from what was later to be called a catholic and critical stance.

To say that the Tractarians had won is certainly not to say that every position which they took and every point of view which they advocated was accepted in the Church of England and in the Anglican Communion. The Evangelical tradition not only still continued as a vital force, but it seriously challenged Anglo-Catholicism on many issues. The victory that Tractarianism won was to transform the Church of England (and by extension the Anglican Communion) into a community which believed itself to be a divinely commissioned body, one called to become a community of people with an apostolate to the world, to the end that all human beings might be united to Christ as incarnate lord. No longer was it a question of proving that the Anglican Church was a part of the Catholic Church; by the time *Lux Mundi* appeared it had become a question of determining what the consequences of Catholicism might be in the life of the Church. The question 'How does the Church live out its Catholic heritage?' is a more serious question than 'Am I a Catholic?' The Tractarians, especially Dr Pusey by his personal witness, had made that more serious question an issue which the Anglican Communion had to face. Because of the Oxford Movement, Anglicans had to ask themselves how their belief in Jesus Christ as incarnate lord affected what they believed about the Church as his presence in the world. The writers of *Lux Mundi* continued that ongoing self-examination, but they were able to attempt it only because of what Tractarianism had begun. For the next generation the theological and pastoral concern facing Anglicanism was no longer defence, but the challenge and opportunity to learn what it means truly to be Catholic.

The other significant feature of *Lux Mundi* was that it

represented a shift in the intellectual concerns of Anglo-Catholicism. In order to defend and justify their doctrinal positions and their convictions about the Church, the Tractarians had looked back to the primitive and undivided Church for the standard and norm in doctrine and polity. But at the end of the nineteenth century and the beginning of the twentieth, new questions arose about the authority of holy scripture, about the possibility of historical development, and about the intellectual foundations of Christian faith which made the Tractarian view untenable. *Lux Mundi* attempted to meet those intellectual challenges by taking the doctrine of the Incarnation as a paradigm for the Church's theological task. In the various essays in *Lux Mundi* the fundamental question was: If in the Incarnation God enters time and history, how can that enable us to understand the temporal and historical life of the Church which is his Body? Can there, in other words, be a legitimate development in the Church's belief and practice? In the preface to *Lux Mundi* Charles Gore stated what was to become the new theological stance for Anglo-Catholicism:

> The real development of theology is . . . the process in which the Church, standing firm in her old truths, enters into the apprehension of the new social and intellectual movements of each age and because 'the truth makes her free', is able to assimilate all new material, to welcome and give its place to all new knowledge, to throw herself into the sanctification of each new social order . . . showing again and again her power of witnessing under changed conditions to the catholic capacity of her faith and life.

Such an incarnational theology enabled the *Lux Mundi* school to meet a variety of challenges to the Christian faith and to provide a new intellectual and theological climate for Anglo-Catholicism. It also enabled theologians to understand the catholicity and apostolicity of the Church in a new way and to broaden the vision of Anglicanism in its ecumenical task.

In the early decades of the twentieth century, to a large degree as a result of *Lux Mundi*, the doctrine of the Incarnation itself became a major theological concern, and the various studies which were written created a new climate within which the catholicity and apostolicity of the Church could be discussed. In Chapter 1 we saw how the Chalcedonian Definition sought to express the doctrine of the Incarnation in a particular way: to affirm without equivocation the humanity and divinity of Christ in the unity of one person, and in doing so to preserve the insights of the Alexandrian and Antiochene schools that the taking of our human nature in the man Jesus by God the Word is the completion of our humanity, not its negation. The unity of the natural and supernatural, temporal and eternal in Christ is the sacramental and incarnational principle of the way in which God works in his creation. Anglican theologians in the early part of the twentieth century explored that incarnational and sacramental principle more deeply, and focused upon the question of the unity of God and man in Jesus Christ and upon the consequences of that unity for the doctrine of the Church. In doing so they were carrying on the tradition which we have already seen in Hooker and in the Tractarians: that the Church and its sacramental life are essentially related to the Incarnation and that they are the means whereby we are made able to participate in the divine life. For the *Lux Mundi* school such a way of thinking meant that the Church in every time and place is the visible and institutional structure through which the spiritual presence of Christ is known and made available in grace to those who believe. In baptism we are incorporated into the body of the incarnate Christ and in the eucharist we are made partakers of his eternal life. The Church is a sacred mystery, the Body of Christ in the world and in history.

Charles Gore, who was certainly one of the most influential theologians of the time, used the phrase 'extension of the Incarnation' in order to express the relationship between the event of the Incarnation and the continuing life of the Church. Even though his way of describing the

Church was criticized by some as being imprecise, nonetheless it had a great influence upon the doctrine of the Church in its time. It is clear that in speaking in such a way he was concerned to convey that the Church and the sacramental life are both grounded in the person of Christ, that they derive their reality from him, and that they are now the visible expression of his presence. Certainly, he did not mean in some odd way that the actual physical body of Jesus Christ was extended in time and space, but rather that the risen and exalted Christ is now actively present in the Church as his Body in a way that is analogous to the presence of the eternal Word in the historical man, Jesus of Nazareth. The visible Church, with its institutional structures, and with the water of baptism and the bread and wine of the eucharist, is an incarnational, sacramental reality, the union of the spiritual and material, of the eternal and temporal.

There is, however, more to the matter than that. The Incarnation speaks not only about the Church but also about human history itself. Gore's theology has been described as the wedding of Tractarianism with the theology of F. D. Maurice, and certainly it was on lines similar to Maurice that the *Lux Mundi* school was able to develop an incarnational theology that had tremendous consequences for Anglicanism. Maurice, a contemporary of the Tractarians and sometimes their opponent (he was sharply criticized by Newman, for example), taught at the University of London and later at Cambridge. In his own day he was regarded as a theological liberal because of his views on baptism and eternal life. His concern to see the significance of Christ in relation to the Kingdom of God which Jesus proclaimed helped later Anglican theologians to see however that the Incarnation is universal in its scope because it speaks of the relationship of all human beings to the Kingdom which is fulfilled in Christ himself. The world, Maurice said, is humanity not yet united in its fullness to Christ; the Church is the sacramental sign and anticipation of that unity with God in Christ which is yet to be. Thus to talk about the Incarnation and the Church is to

46

talk about the fullness of Christ when in him all people are gathered into the divine life. In the Incarnation God has created a new humanity, a new relationship with himself. The Incarnation is at the centre of the world as well as at the centre of the Church. To speak of the Catholic Church in such a context meant for Maurice that it was not to be identified with any present reality or particular ecclesiastical body. Catholicity means the fullness of Christ when he is all in all and humanity has been restored to its relationship with God; it is a hope yet to be realized and completed.

In this theological context, Anglican theologians in the first half of the twentieth century reflected much more deeply upon the significance of the doctrine of the Incarnation for the Catholicity of the Church than had the Tractarians. The fruit of their reflections can be seen chiefly in two areas. First, they were able to make a connection between the Church as an institutional, visible body in the world and the process of historical development in matters of doctrine and polity and, by doing so, to show how change and development were possible without a loss of continuity with the past. Second, they came to see that Catholicism means comprehensiveness, not exclusion, and that this in turn meant taking seriously the fragmentation of the Catholic Church. To do so led to the necessity of developing an ecumenical theology of the Catholic Church as a hope yet to be realized. All I can do here is to give an indication of the many contributions made by Anglicans to an ecumenical theology during the first half of the present century, for the period includes the major work of, among others, L. S. Thornton, O. C. Quick and William Temple, and the early work of Michael Ramsey, each of whom deserves a special study. To the degree that I can briefly suggest the main lines of development, we shall be able to discover a foundation upon which Anglican ecumenical theology must build at the present time and in the future.

Christianity claims to be a historical religion. By that we usually mean two things: that Christian faith is founded upon certain events in history to which the New Testament

47

bears witness, and that the Church is an institution in history even while claiming a supernatural, supra-historical reality. Tractarianism, like most other Christian theologies prior to the nineteenth century, did not explore the significance of the historical dimension of the Church and its possible consequences for doctrine and polity. As we have seen, the Tractarians looked to the first centuries of the Church's life as having fixed once and for all the credal formulations of Christian faith and the institutional structures of the Church. *Lux Mundi* opened up new perspectives for Anglicanism as had other theological writings for some of the Protestant Churches. Newman's theological writings on development were eventually to effect a similar change in Roman Catholicism. With a greater appreciation for historical change and development it became possible for the *Lux Mundi* essayists to think of the Church as the continuing, active presence of Christ in history, an incarnational presence in fact, and so to develop a more dynamic theology. The Catholic Church, as the continuation of the Incarnation, could, while maintaining continuity with its past, be open to the Spirit's movement in history, leading the Church into truth. In other words, if the centre of the Catholic Church as a visible and historical institution is Christ himself, the incarnate Word and Son, then Christian people need not fear historical change: Christ is present in history with his Body, the Church. In one of his later writings Dr Pusey had spoken of the humility of God in coming to us and taking our nature to himself. In the twentieth century Anglican theology began to grasp the deeper implications of that incarnational presence, namely, that in the Incarnation God commits himself to our history, not just as an event in the past, but always. The doctrine of Incarnation speaks of the humility of the God who has entered history without reservation and who lives in it now in the Church.

Such a sense of catholicity can welcome development and change, even while not always approving their course, because of the way in which it perceives the relationship of the Church to the incarnate lord. Not only did such a view deepen the awareness of Christ's sacramental presence in Christian spirituality, it also enabled some of the leading Anglo-Catholic theologians in the twentieth century to confront the many challenges which were being made to Christian faith and practice. They approached the modern world not in a spirit of rejection but in a spirit of synthesis because they believed in the working of God in Christ through history. Perhaps the best expression of the strength of this movement in Anglicanism is to be found in the preface to another group of essays which, while they went beyond *Lux Mundi*, nonetheless carried forward its incarnational theology. In the preface to *Essays Catholic and Critical*, published in 1932, the editor, E. G. Selwyn, wrote:

> The two terms Catholic and critical represent principles, habits, and tempers of the religious mind which only reach their maturity in combination. To the first belongs everything in us that acknowledges and adores the one abiding, transcendent, and supremely given reality God; that believes in Jesus Christ, as the unique revelation in true personal form of His Mystery; and recognizes His Spirit embodied in the Church as the authoritative and ever-living witness of His Will, word, and work. To the second belongs the exercise of that divinely implanted gift of reason by which we measure, sift, examine, and judge whatever is proposed for our belief, whether it be a theological doctrine or a statement of historical fact, and so establish, deepen, and purify our understanding of the truth of the Gospel.[1]

Many of the conclusions reached by the writers of *Essays Catholic and Critical* are ones with which not everyone might now agree, but the method there proposed remains a viable expression of an incarnational theology for Anglican Catholicism. It takes with utmost seriousness the divine presence in human history in a way that can allow for the Church's search for truth under the lordship of Christ through the Spirit.

One of the most important corollaries to such a perception of Catholicism was that it enabled Anglican theology to have a wider and more comprehensive understanding of the Church itself than had been possible for the Tractarians. Tractarianism had attempted to justify the Catholic claims of Anglicanism by identifying it as one of the branches of the Catholic Church, the other two being the Roman and the Orthodox. Since these other two branches did not accept such a theory, each regarding itself as the only true Catholic Church, the branch theory created an anomalous position for Anglicanism. In the twentieth century, however, Anglicans became involved in, and indeed were the leaders of, the movement to restore visible unity to the universal Church of Christ, not only unity with Rome and Orthodoxy but also with the churches of the Reformation. They could do this because developing within Anglicanism was the beginning of an ecumenical theology for the Catholic Church. In this development can be seen evidence of Maurice's influence on Anglo-Catholicism. Maurice, as I have said, had spoken of a future Catholicism, one which was yet to be fulfilled, and he had refused to identify the Catholic Church with any existing ecclesiastical society. No one church could claim to be the Catholic Church, but all churches contained in themselves elements of catholicity which would find their completion only in the coming fullness of the Church. For Maurice, to be baptized into Christ was to be incorporated into the Catholic Church no matter what division might at present separate the ecclesiastical bodies in Christendom. Bishop Gore had dealt in a similar way with the idea of Catholicism. For him, to be Catholic meant to be comprehensive, to hold together even in conflict the traditional signs of the Catholic Church (creeds, ministry, and sacraments) with the witness of the Reformation Churches to biblical authority and the freedom of conscience. Only through such comprehensiveness, he believed, could a true catholicity emerge in Christianity, one which would look not to an infallible voice (it should be remembered that the dogma of papal infallibility had been proclaimed in the nineteenth century) but to the converging authority of scripture, church tradition and human reason.

On such a foundation other Anglican theologians were able to explore more deeply the meaning of division within the one Church of Christ. Division came to be seen not simply as a separation between true and false, Catholic and Protestant, established and free, but as a schism within the Church such that no single ecclesiastical group could claim to be the One, Holy, Catholic and Apostolic Church of the creeds. All were in some degree defective and wanting. Hence a Catholic theology of ecumenism, theologians came to believe, had to be able to grapple more significantly with the *fact* of division in the Church, while maintaining the continuity of the Church with its apostolic foundation. An initial attempt was made by the Lambeth Conference in 1920. The bishops at Lambeth issued an 'Appeal to All Christian People' which began: 'We acknowledge all those who believe in our Lord Jesus Christ, and have been baptized into the name of the Holy Trinity, as sharing with us membership in the universal Church of Christ which is his Body.'

N. P. Williams, writing in 1933, in commemoration of the hundredth anniversary of the beginning of the Oxford Movement, commented on the appeal in a way which had come to characterize how many Anglo-Catholic theologians understood the nature of Catholicity and the role of Anglicanism in the ecumenical movement. He said:

> If, with the Lambeth Conference, we are prepared to use 'the universal Church' of the wider circle of Christendom, it will be natural to reserve the phrase 'the Catholic Church' for the inner circle, or nucleus of Christians possessing both the Apostolic ministry and doctrinal orthodoxy. . . . It is, perhaps, hardly necessary to point out that the reunion with the 'nucleus', of Christians whose faith or order may be deemed to be defective, from the point of view of 'Christian antiquity', is likely to be facilitated by the use of a terminology which does not represent such reunion as a transition from darkness to light but rather as a passage from light to more light.[2]

The language of 'inner' and 'outer' circles is not, perhaps, that which we would use today, but the sense that the reunion of Christendom within the Catholic Church of Christ involves comprehensiveness rather than exclusion or submission had come to be characteristic of much Anglican ecumenical theology before the Second World War. While the problem of orthodoxy in matters of faith would continue to vex Anglicans and other Christians in future generations, Anglicans had come to see that the apostolic ministry represented a distinct contribution which their tradition could make to the one Church. The reason for that derives from a history which has caused Anglicans, perhaps more deeply than any other Christian body, to reflect upon and even to cherish the apostolic ministry of the episcopate in the life of the Church.

Running through the writings of those theologians who have emphasized the Catholic heritage of Anglicanism from the time of Hooker to the Anglo-Catholics of the present century has been a common theme: the providential preservation of the apostolic ministry through the episcopate in the Church of England. While from a strictly historical point of view it may often seem that its preservation was accidental or simply a consequence of the Anglo-Saxon resistance to change, nonetheless the fact that it has been preserved has played an important part in Anglican self-consciousness. What the preservation of the apostolic ministry in the episcopate meant and how it is important for us has been seen differently at different times. For Hooker and the Caroline divines it established the continuity of the Church of England with the ancient Catholic Church prior to the Reformation controversies (even though Hooker himself and some of the Caroline divines were careful to acknowledge the spiritual legitimacy of those churches of the Reformation which had *not* preserved episcopacy). For others it came to mean much more; it represented the assurance and guarantee that the Church of England and other churches in the Anglican Communion were truly a part of the Catholic Church and that the sacramental acts of their ministers were truly linked to the intention and acts of Christ and the apostles. In chapter 2 we saw how the Tractarians used the doctrine of the historic episcopate in this way: they linked it always to the eucharist and they saw it as a defence of the Church's divine commission against the encroachments of the State. What was unfortunate in Tractarianism (although historically it can be understood) was the isolation of the doctrine of the historic episcopate from a broader view of Catholicity, which led to an undue emphasis upon the validity of orders.

While that view continued to be held by some Anglo-Catholics (as it does even now), the historical and theological work of the first half of the present century by others in the Anglo-Catholic tradition helped to clarify and even purify why Anglicans believe the apostolic ministry in the episcopate is of such importance. Without too great an over-simplification their insight can, I think, be expressed thus: it is not a valid ministry which makes a particular ecclesiastical community 'Catholic', nor, on the other hand, the Church which makes the ministry valid; far from being independent of one another, they co-exist: the Catholic Church and the apostolic ministry are inseparably joined in Christ himself. These Anglo-Catholics were thus able to continue to develop the theology of the Church as the Body of Christ, the incarnate lord. I want here simply to indicate some of the themes in the work which was done during this period that are especially important for the future of an ecumenical theology in Anglicanism.

In the first place historical scholarship by Anglicans and others in the twentieth century clarified certain aspects of the development of the apostolic ministry in the Church. To some degree, the Tractarians, in their zeal for the historic episcopate, romanticized history. They thought that the transition from the ministry of the apostles to the episcopal office as it later is found in the Church had been a simple process of passing on apostolic authority in succession by the laying on of hands. Hence they could identify the episcopate as it had come to be in the second century with the institution of the apostles by Christ himself. This meant, of course, that the form of Apostolic Ministry in the episcopate was a matter of divine revelation and ordinance, to depart from which was to depart from the authority and intention of Christ. With deeper historical investigation, however, such a simple view became untenable. While there clearly is a distinct relationship between the apostolic commission of Christ and the later development of episcopacy in the early Church, the nature of that relationship is more complex than formerly realized. Indeed the attempt to prove apostolic succession has, more often than not, resulted in regarding the apostolic ministry as a subject for archaeological investigation and polemical defence, rather than as the sacramental sign of the continuity of the Church in every age with the apostolic Church.

Now it became possible to see that in the ministry of the Church, just as in doctrine, there had been historical development, with some false starts and anomalies, certainly, but that the Church had been guided by the Spirit to a form of ministry which could best carry out the commission of Christ to the apostles. The essential features of apostolic ministry as it must exist in the Catholic Church at any time could then be distinguished from the various ways in which it may have been adapted to local circumstances, such as in the feudal period when the exercise of episcopacy in the Church became confused with secular power. What historical investigation showed to be essential was that the apostolic ministry of oversight (*episcope*) and pastoral care devolved upon a group of human beings in whom the authority of Christ continued for the Church. By the end of the second century the exercise of oversight and pastoral care had become identified with the episcopal office and with the continuing succession in office of those who carried out the apostolic commission. As the Church had to fight against various heretical movements (especially gnosticism, which claimed a secret teaching given by Christ to certain select apostles), the idea of succession in the episcopal office became increasingly important: the bishop could trace his authority in doctrine and practice to the apostles themselves and so he in his person was a denial of any secret or heretical teaching. Certainly as the church spread throughout the Roman Empire many new functions were taken on by the bishops as the 'successors of the apostles', but their most essential function remained the care of the churches and the carrying out of Christ's commission to preach the Gospel to all people.

Thus through the historical investigations carried out in the twentieth century the episcopal office came to be seen as having a sacramental and institutional significance greater than that of simply providing a justification for the transferral of power, and with this came a recognition that the changes which had occurred in the history of its development might well have dimmed the clearer perception of its essential ministry in the Church. There were consequences, too, for the way in which Anglicans came to see the importance of the apostolic ministry in relation to those churches of the Reformation in which the episcopate had not been preserved, either by historical accident or by having been intentionally rejected. It became necessary to look behind the controversies of the Reformation and attempt to discover what it was in the early Church which had in fact led to that form of ministry which Anglicanism itself had maintained. In an essay published in one of the more influential volumes dealing with the question, *The Apostolic Ministry*, edited by Bishop Kirk of Oxford, Dom Gregory Dix saw the problem clearly. He wrote that a defence of apostolic succession and the larger question of the apostolic ministry had to be undertaken in such a way as not to illegitimate the ministries of other churches, namely by discerning the reasons why the ministry had developed in a particular way during the early period of the Church's life and so discovering those principles which could guide us in dealing with the problems raised by the Reformation controversies today. 'The first concern of Christian historical study,' he said, 'is not to extract precedents from the Christian past to bind or justify the Christian present, but to understand why the Christian past took the particular form it did.'[3]

The beginning of an ecumenical theology in Anglicanism,

especially in reference to the ministry, manifested itself in that movement for Christian unity undertaken by the bishops of the Anglican Communion in the Lambeth conferences in the first five decades of this century. The movement had begun with the Chicago/Lambeth Quadrilateral in 1888, which had called for a reunion of Christendom on the basis of a fourfold agreement: the authority of Holy Scripture; the Apostles' Creed; the two sacraments of baptism and the supper of the lord; and the historic episcopate. Without question it was the last of these, the historic episcopate, which caused the greatest difficulty for other Christian churches. The non-episcopal churches wanted to know what Anglicans meant by it and how they understood it in relation to the ministries of other churches, and their questioning more and more forced Anglicans to clarify for themselves why they have regarded the historic episcopate as so central to the expression of apostolic ministry.

What I believe is most significant in many of the theological writings of this period, and in the official statements made by the Lambeth Conferences and other authoritative bodies in the Anglican Communion, is the distinction which came to be made between apostolic ministry and the historic episcopate. Now it was possible to say more clearly that apostolic ministry is the fundamental ministry which derives from Christ himself as the High Priest who reconciles the world to God through his life, death and resurrection, and whose ministry of reconciliation is carried on in the Church. The General Convention of the Episcopal Church in the United States, meeting in 1949, adopted a statement which sums up much Anglican thinking on the subject during the previous decades of ecumenical involvement. The 'Statement of Faith and Order' which they adopted says:

The Church as the Body of Christ, sharing His Life, has a ministerial function derived from that of Christ. In this function every member has his place and share according to his different capabilities and calling. The

Church is set before us in the New Testament as a body of believers having within it, as its recognized focus of unity, of teaching and authority, the Apostolate, which owed its origin to the action of the Lord himself. There was not first an Apostolate which gathered a body of believers about itself; nor was there a completely structureless collection of believers which gave authority to the Apostles to speak and act on its behalf. From the first there was the fellowship of believers finding its unity in the Twelve. Thus the New Testament bears witness to the principle of a distinctive ministry, as an original element, but not the sole constitutive element in the life of the Church.[4]

The Statement, which had been approved by the Lambeth Conference of 1948, reflects the growing theological consensus in Anglican theology that the apostolic ministry is not limited to one particular ecclesiastical organization nor to one particular confession of faith. Rather, it is made up of all those who through baptism are united to the Catholic Church and so to Christ himself. Apostolic ministry, therefore, ought not to be identified *exclusively* with one historical form of ministry, nor should a particular form be used as the means for denying legitimacy to the ministry of other churches. The true ministry of the Catholic Church, as it extends through all ages and places, is ultimately the ministry of Christ expressed in his apostolic commission to the Church as his Body. Only in the fullness of catholicity, in a truly united Church, shall we be able once again to speak of the fullness of the ministry. The task of the ecumenical movement is, through the Spirit, to bring that about.

But Anglican formularies and most Anglican theologians in this period went on to assert that the way in which apostolic ministry has been most adequately expressed in the Church's life and the form for which there is the greatest authority is the historic episcopate. To say that the historic episcopate, as a reality in the Church's life from the end of the second century, was a consequence of development in the primitive Church is not to deny that it was of divine authority, as the Spirit guided the Church to find that form of ministry most appropriate to its life and mission. As the 'Statement on Faith and Order' went on to say, Anglicans have found in the historic episcopate, in spite of all the accretions which have sometimes obscured its function for Christian people, a visible sign of the Church's continuity with the apostles and a personal sign of the Church's unity. It has in other words become a sacramental sign of the unity of the Church, with Christ as the high priest and chief shepherd of the Church. Understood in this way the historic episcopate can, in the words of the Lambeth Appeal, offer to a divided Christendom 'a ministry acknowledged by every part of the Church as possessing not only the inward call of the Spirit, but also the commission of Christ and the authority of the whole Body' in order that the whole Church gathered together as one family may offer the Eucharist as its worship and service.[5] In a very real sense one can say that the best intentions of the Tractarians, when they saw the essential relationship between the eucharist and ministry, had been fulfilled.

4 Unity and the Roman Catholic Church

In the first three chapters of this book I have dealt with the historical and theological development of that movement in the Anglican Communion which has been called Anglo-Catholicism and shown how, carrying on the work of the Oxford Movement, it represented the regaining of a vision of the Church in which the doctrine of the Incarnation was of fundamental importance. That vision had consequences in many areas of the Church's life, but its most important consequence, I believe, has been the deepening of Anglican understanding about the catholicity and apostolicity of the Church, first in reference to Anglicanism itself and later in reference to those other churches from which it is separated. In the first half of the twentieth century Anglicans began to develop an ecumenical theology in which their understanding of the centrality of the Incarnation to the nature of the Church enabled them to appropriate more seriously in their own lives the unity of all Christians in Christ and hence created a greater desire for the visible unity of Christ's Church. To see the Church as an incarnational reality because it is the continuing presence of the risen and exalted Christ in the world led many Anglicans to oppose any sectarian spirit which would 'unchurch' those who have been baptized into Christ. It has taken much time and theological reflection for Anglicanism to come to such an awareness and to understand the implications of what began in the Oxford Movement, but that journey in faith has represented the best of the Anglo-Catholic movement: to make the vision of the Church which had its origin in the *Tracts for the Times* the heritage and responsibility of all Anglicans. Now, I believe, it can truly be said that the future calling of Anglicanism is its work for the visible unity of the Church, and in that calling Anglo-Catholicism has a particular role to play and a witness to maintain.

To develop an ecumenical theology and to put that theology into practice can be two completely different things. The history of the ecumenical movement in this century has been replete with attempts at unity which have got nowhere or which have led to even greater schism within the churches involved. In the United States, for example, where there is a long history of cultural and religious pluralism, some of the attempts to bring together even those churches with a common theological tradition have foundered because of ethnic differences and have resulted in certain groups refusing to be absorbed into a larger denomination. Even more, when the desire for unity has arisen chiefly out of sentimentality or the practical considerations of finance and strategy, without serious theological and cultural differences being faced, further fragmentation has sometimes resulted. The theological, spiritual and cultural heritage of a people cannot be taken lightly or dismissed as irrelevant.

With all the difficulties involved, however, Anglicans throughout the world have pursued their ecumenical vocation in a variety of ways. In this chapter and the next I shall examine several current conversations with other Churches. They illustrate the advances that can be made and the problems that still remain. In each case the claim of Anglicans to be a part of the Catholic Church and to continue the apostolic ministry in the episcopate has been central. And, as one might expect of a church which sees itself as a *via media*, those conversations have looked in several directions.

Conversations with the Roman Catholic Church are taking place at the international level and have involved the whole Anglican Communion, and they also involve Anglicans with a church which claims strict continuity with the ancient church and which would define catholicity and apostolicity in terms of its own tradition. The others with which I shall be concerned are taking place at the provincial level. They involve churches which would in some way, although the ways differ, identify themselves with the Reformation or with other reform movements in Christian history. Of these latter movements towards unity, from which we are learning much, I shall say something in chapter 5. Here I want to deal with what I believe to be the most important and difficult aspect of the conversations with the Roman Catholic Church – the nature of apostolic ministry.

Even though many of the early Tracts were highly polemical towards Roman claims, reunion with Rome (and also with Orthodoxy) was one of the early hopes of the Oxford Movement, and it has continued to be a hope for Anglo-Catholicism. The reason for this is obvious: those who would call themselves Anglo-Catholics can clearly identify more easily with a church with which they appear to share a common sacramental spirituality, a doctrine of the apostolic ministry and a concern for tradition and continuity in doctrine. With Rome, however, the path to reunion has been difficult, and it is even yet not clear what reunion between the two churches might mean. Some things have become apparent in both a positive and a negative way. The establishment of international and provincial commissions to discuss doctrinal and pastoral issues has enabled both sides to see more clearly what they have in common and what areas of disagreement still exist. Even more important, the spontaneous growth of societies for common prayer and, to the degree possible, public worship is slowly but surely bringing to an end some of the old hostilities and suspicions. Anglicans and Roman Catholics are beginning through common prayer together to discover the unity of their faith at a level deeper than doctrinal formulations and institutional structures.

At the international level a spectacular and well publicized achievement has been the doctrinal consensus reached between Anglicans and the Roman Catholic Church. The Anglican/Roman Catholic International Commission (ARCIC), initiated by Pope Paul VI and Archbishop

Michael Ramsey to explore the issues which divide the two churches and to discover what they hold in common, issued in March 1982 *The Final Report*, containing the Agreed Statements and Elucidations on the Eucharist, Ministry and Ordination, and Authority in the Church. ARCIC has arrived at such a significant degree of theological consensus as to encourage the hope among many that further steps towards visible unity can now be taken, even though many serious problems still remain. Indeed, that hope was further encouraged by the joint statement of the Archbishop of Canterbury and Pope John Paul at Canterbury Cathedral in May 1982. At the provincial level equally significant, although less well publicized, advances have been made. In the United States, for example, the Anglican-Roman Catholic Consultation (ARC), which began its work in 1965, has stated as its goal the realization of full communion between the two churches, and it has issued a series of agreed statements on doctrine and on certain pastoral questions which affect both. In 1977 ARC issued a report on its twelve years of work, 'Where We Are: A Challenge for the Future', in which it cited such substantial agreement between the two churches in the United States that it could refer to them as 'sister churches' in the one Church of Christ.

The amazing growth of consensus between the two churches is, of course, the result of many factors: the personality of Pople John XXIII, the Second Vatican Council, the courage of Archbishop Geoffrey Fisher, who was the first Archbishop of Canterbury since the Reformation to make a formal visit to the Holy See, and the later visit of Archbishop Michael Ramsey to Pope Paul VI. But it has also become possible because of significant developments in Roman Catholic theology which have paralleled those developments in Anglicanism discussed in chapter 3. Many Roman Catholic and Anglican theologians now approach ecumenical theology in a very similar way and this has resulted in a theological climate considerably different from the one which prevailed in the last century or even earlier in this century. Indeed, I believe it can be said that the form of ecumenical theology which lies behind the *Final Report* has consequences for Anglicans in all of their conversations with other churches as they carry out their vocation to work for the unity of the Church. It is essential, therefore, to say something about the form of ecumenical theology which has developed among many Anglicans and Roman Catholics.

In 1972 the Anglican-Roman Catholic Consultation in the United States issued a study on 'Doctrinal Agreement and Christian Unity: Methodological Considerations'.[1] The study was in response to the Malta Report of the Anglican-Roman Catholic Joint Preparatory Commission (1968) which prepared the ground for ARCIC. Section 5 of the Malta Report was especially important because it established the principles by which ARCIC would work:

> We agree that revealed Truth is given in Holy Scripture and formulated in dogmatic definitions through thought-forms and language which are historically conditioned. We are encouraged by the growing agreement of theologians of our two Communions on methods of interpreting this historical transmission of revelation. We should examine further and together both the way in which we assent to and apprehend dogmatic truths and the legitimate means of understanding and interpreting them theologically. Although we agree that doctrinal comprehensiveness must have its limits, we believe that diversity has an intrinsic value when used creatively rather than destructively.[2]

The study issued by ARC in response to the Malta Report begins by acknowledging as a basic theological principle that the transcendent mystery of God can never be fully and completed expressed in human language. Every doctrinal statement is conditioned by the particular situation out of which human beings speak − the historical and cultural circumstances of an age as well as the philosophical, psychological and linguistic presuppositions of those who are seeking to formulate what they believe to be true. The

63

study recognizes the possibility of historical development in doctrine when it says: 'Because encounter with God always calls man beyond himself it must be recognized that all religious expression may itself be transcended. The abiding presence of the Holy Spirit moves communities of believers to express their life in Christ in ways that may not be abstractly deducible from their previous statements.' In addition, partly because of the nature of all theological statement and partly because of a history of separation between church communities, there can be legitimate differences in the expression of a common faith and different ways through which an ecclesial community can understand itself in relation to Christ. On that foundation the study then offers six principles by means of which participants in ecumenical conversations can assess divergent formulations of doctrine in order to discover their common faith underneath the divergences. They are:

1 Paradoxical tension: the ambiguity in all theological statements because of the inadequacy of human language to encompass the divine mystery.
2 Contextual transfer: the need to find new language and concepts to express a truth of Christian belief.
3 Relative emphasis: that certain doctrines from the past may no longer be considered as crucial to our salvation as was once thought.
4 Doctrinal pluralism: that there can be legitimate diversity in the interpretation of doctrine within a single church and that the same mystery of faith can find different expression in different groups of Christians.
5 Empathetic evaluation: that certain doctrinal formulations play a different role in different communities, so that a serious attempt must be made to understand what a particular doctrinal formulation is expressing in the life of another community.
6 Responsive listening: that every church must be open to hear criticism from others about what in its own tradition needs clarification and modification.

The study concludes in a way that is particularly significant for the kind of incarnational theology which we have found developing in Anglicanism:

> Mindful of the fact that the revelation once for all given to man is the person of Christ present in the Spirit, Christians are called to be faithful to that presence at all times in their living tradition. The foregoing principles should be applied in conformity to that abiding presence, and thus in a way that leads to an ever richer appropriation of the gospel.[3]

The influence of such a methodology can be seen throughout the agreed statements issued by ARCIC, as well as in other ecumenical documents. I want, however, to focus here upon what is, I believe, the central issue between Anglicans and Roman Catholics, the doctrine of the ministry and the exercise of ministerial authority, in order to see how such a methodology has made possible the convergence of our thinking on the ministry while at the same time helping us to recognize the problems which continue to separate us.

In 1973 ARCIC issued its *Agreed Statement on Ministry and Ordination* — the Canterbury Statement — and in 1979 some elucidations on that Statement. The Statement itself is clearly not intended to be a complete treatise on the doctrine of the ministry, but it enunciates those beliefs about the ministry which Anglicans and Roman Catholics believe to be central. What is said in the Statement represents for Anglicans a continuation of that way of thinking about the ministry which had begun earlier in the century; for Roman Catholics it represents a different approach from that which characterized much Roman Catholic thinking prior to Vatican II. The Statement also reflects much of the theological and historical work that has been done in other, non-episcopal traditions, even though it assumes that Anglicans and Roman Catholics regard their pattern of ordained ministry to be in some way fundamental to any considerations about the ministry.

The Statement quite rightly begins by locating the doctrine of the ministry, whether ordained or not, in the relationship of Christ to his Church. As Christ himself in the Incarnation expresses perfectly what it is to be the servant of God and man, so the ministry of the Church exists primarily as the way in which Christian people carry out the reconciling and sanctifying service of Christ. In that sense we can speak of the apostolic foundation of the Church:

> All Christian apostolate originates in the sending of the Son by the Father. The Church is apostolic not only because its faith and life must reflect the witness to Jesus Christ given in the early Church by the apostles, but also because it is charged to continue in the apostles' commission to communicate to the world what it has received. Within the whole history of mankind the Church is to be the community of reconciliation.[4]

Within the context of understanding apostolicity as carrying on the ministry of reconciliation, the Statement is also able to allow for the historical development of the ordained ministry in the New Testament period and in the next century and a half. The Statement compares the historical development of the ordained ministry to the canon of Holy Scripture: 'Just as the formation of the canon of the New Testament was a process incomplete until the second half of the second century, so also the full emergence of the threefold ministry of bishop, presbyter and deacon required a longer period than the apostolic age. Thereafter this threefold structure became universal in the Church.' (Canterbury Statement, sec. 6.) As the ministry of the whole Church is grounded in the ministry of Christ himself, so the ordained ministry developed to carry out the ministry of the Church in a particular way. In the Elucidation (1979) the relationship of the ordained ministry to the priesthood of the whole people of God and to the priesthood of Christ himself is stated precisely: the ordained ministry 'exists for the service of all the faithful' (Canterbury Statement, sec. 2).

The Statement goes on to say that in the New Testament itself there are various images through which the ordained ministry is described, but its essential function is oversight (*episcope*) in the community, joined with the ministry of word and sacrament. While the Statement does not spell out the form which *episcope* can take in the Church, it does clearly identify the ministry of word and sacrament, and especially the priestly offering of the eucharist, with those who by ordination exercise oversight in the Church. Because the eucharist is the central act of the Church's reconciling mission to the world, 'it is right that he who has oversight in the church and is the focus of its unity should preside at the celebration of the eucharist' (Canterbury Statement, sec. 12). The ordained ministry is thus appropriately described in terms of priesthood because in it the priestly role of Christ is reflected. 'Because the eucharist is the memorial of the sacrifice of Christ, the action of the presiding minister in reciting again the words of Christ at the last supper and distributing to the assembly the holy gifts is seen to stand in a sacramental relation to what Christ himself did in offering his own sacrifice' (Canterbury Statement, sec. 13).

Perhaps the most important section of the Statement, in the light of Anglican concerns about the ordained ministry, is that on vocation and ordination. From the Oxford Movement and further theological reflection on the ordained ministry has arisen a strong witness on the part of Anglo-Catholicism to the sacramentality of holy orders. However, that view has not always been held by all Anglicans, and the Statement, therefore, quite rightly refers to Article XXV of the Articles of Religion as reflecting some reservations among Anglicans on this question. Article XXV distinguishes between the two sacraments of the gospel — baptism and the supper of the Lord — and the five commonly called sacraments, of which the ordained ministry is one. The Statement itself clearly reflects that tradition in Anglicanism which understands ordination as a distinct setting apart in the ministry of Christ.

In this sacramental act, the gift of God is bestowed upon the ministers, with the promise of divine grace for their work and sanctification. . . . Just as Christ has united the Church inseparably with himself, and as God calls all the faithful to lifelong discipleship, so the gifts and calling of God to the ministers are irrevocable. For this reason, ordination is unrepeatable in both our churches. (Canterbury Statement, sec. 11)

In the Elucidation that statement is strengthened by defining the rite of ordination as 'a visible sign through which the grace of God is given by the Holy Spirit in the Church. . . . Those who are ordained by prayer and the laying on of hands receive their ministry from Christ through those designated in the Church to hand it on; together with the office they are given the grace needed for its fulfillment' (Elucidation, 1979, sec. 3).

Finally, the Statement gives expression to that point of view on the episcopate which Anglicanism has come to understand through its own theological reflection:

In the ordination of a new bishop, other bishops lay hands on him, as they request the gift of the Spirit for his ministry and receive him into their ministerial fellowship. Because they are entrusted with the oversight of other churches, this participation in his ordination signifies that this new bishop and his church are within the communion of churches. Moreover, because they are representatives of their churches in fidelity to the teaching and mission of the apostles and are members of the episcopal college their participation also ensures the historical continuity of this church with the apostolic Church and of its bishop with the original apostolic ministry. The communion of the churches in mission, faith, and holiness, through time and space is thus symbolized and maintained in the bishop. Here are comprised the essential features of what is meant in our two traditions by ordination in apostolic succession (Canterbury Statement, sec. 11).

The Canterbury Statement and the Elucidation both conclude by stating that the consensus which has been reached would suggest that the question of Anglican orders should be re-examined in the new context of doctrinal agreement. Here they are giving expression to a hope which was raised in the Malta Report that the 'validity' of Anglican orders could be examined anew in the broader context of a theology of the Church and ministry (Malta Report, sec. 19). The Elucidation also raises the question, to which I shall return, of the ordination of women in some parts of the Anglican Communion, which by that time had taken place.

I have quoted extensively from the Canterbury Statement because I believe it to be a most significant document, not only for Anglican/Roman Catholic traditions but also for conversations between Anglicans and other churches who do not share the same understanding of the ordained ministry and apostolic orders. By placing that problem in a new context for Anglicans and Roman Catholics, the Statement may enable Anglicans to offer their understanding of the ministry to other churches in a new way. The Statement significantly carries forward the development of Anglican thinking in this very difficult area.

There is, however, an area of disagreement found not only among Roman Catholics but among some Anglicans as well: whether there can be legitimate development of doctrine and polity through history. In 1982 the Sacred Congregation for the Doctrine of the Faith in Rome issued a doctrinal analysis of the several Statements and Elucidations produced by ARCIC. The Sacred Congregation found serious deficiencies in all of the Statements, even while acknowledging that some advance had been made. Their criticism of the Canterbury Statement, however, is of particular importance because it takes sharp issue with the methodology adopted by ARCIC. In criticizing the section on the sacramentality of ordination and its failure to state clearly that the sacrament of holy orders was instituted by Christ himself, the Sacred Congregation remarks:

> It may be noted here that the question bearing on the institution of the sacraments and on the way in which this can be known is intimately linked to the question of the interpretation of Holy Scripture. The fact of institution cannot be considered only within the limits of the certitude arrived at by the historical method; one must take into account the authentic interpretation of the scriptures which it pertains to the church to make.[5]

ARCIC was quite clearly following the theological methodology established by the Malta Report and, at least implicitly, the elaboration of that methodology by the ARC study. The methodology argued for a recognition that all doctrinal statements are conditioned by the historical circumstances of human beings in their attempt to express the mystery of God. It is a good example of an incarnational approach to theology, as I have called it, because it takes into account the divine and human dimensions of the Church as it seeks to express its faith in the ambiguous conditions of human history. In the earlier 'Agreed Statement on Eucharistic Doctrine' (Windsor, 1971), such an approach had enabled ARCIC to reach a theological consensus on many of the questions which had divided Anglicans and Roman Catholics for centuries, by discovering our common belief about the eucharist beneath the diversity of formulations and historical developments in the two churches. In the Canterbury Statement, that methodology was applied specifically to the vexed question of the ordained ministry. By recognizing the diversity of images and concepts used in the New Testament for describing the ministry, and the different patterns of ministry which emerged in the primitive church, the Statement was able to argue that the form which the ordained ministry took by the end of the second century could be understood as a legitimate expression of the ministry of Christ. In other words, what Christ instituted was not a particular structure of ministry, but an apostolate and ministry to the world which the Church, guided by the Spirit, expressed in the ordained ministry of bishops, priests and deacons. The Sacred Congregation, taking a more static view of revelation and institution, would appear to be arguing that the particular structure of the ordained ministry was revealed to the Church in a way that admits of no historical development or diversity. Such a point of view makes it difficult, if not impossible, to account for historical evidence and to allow for diversity in the ways through which the one ministry of Christ, into which all Christians enter through their baptism, can be expressed in different traditions and in different historical circumstances. On the contrary, it maintains that all diversity − whether in doctrine or polity − must conform to Roman Catholic tradition as defined by the infallible teaching authority of the Church. This disagreement has implications of considerable importance for two vexing problems which face Anglicans and Roman Catholics: papal authority and the ordination of women.

The 'Windsor Statement' on Authority in the Church II (1981) was an attempt to reach a consensus on the fundamental issue between Anglicanism and Roman Catholicism: the status of the papacy. Certainly no other question has been more divisive in the history of Anglican and Roman Catholic relations. It was first raised by ARCIC in the 'Venice Statement' on Authority in the Church I (1976), but many felt that the crucial issues had not been addressed with sufficient precision in that Statement. The Venice Statement was, however, of considerable importance because it provided a theological foundation for the discussion in the Windsor Statement (1981) of the major issues of the authority of Scripture for papal claims, the language of 'divine right', papal infallibility and papal jurisdiction. The method followed in the Venice Statement was that which we have analysed in some detail concerning the ministry. First there was the recognition that all authority in the Church derives from Christ himself as he through the Spirit dwells in the Christian community (the

71

koinonia). The authority of Christ is mediated through human beings as they carry out the mission of the Church in the world. The Statement then discusses the various structures and institutions through which the authority of Christ has been mediated historically to the Church: scripture, *episcope*, general and provincial councils, and the faithful response of Christian people to the Spirit. In this process of discerning the authority of Christ the Church is shaped by its history and experience and by its faithfulness to the gospel (Venice Statement, sec. 15). Only in such a context can we understand the exercise of primacy in the Church: 'If primacy is to be a genuine expression of *episcope* it will foster the *koinonia* by helping the bishops in their task of apostolic leadership both in their local church and in the Church universal' (Venice Statement, sec. 21).

In the subsequent discussion of papal claims, in the Venice Statement, the Elucidation to the Venice Statement (1981) and then in the fuller discussion in the Windsor Statement (1981), it becomes obvious that ARCIC is putting forward a twofold argument, one which would be acceptable to Anglicans, who have rejected papal claims, and to Roman Catholics, who have perhaps claimed too much. The argument is that the universal primacy of oversight in the Church is to be understood as fundamental to God's plan for the Church in its mission, but that the way in which the exercise of that universal primacy has been exercised has developed and can continue to do so in the history of the Church. As is said in the Elucidation: 'But the way *episcope* is realized concretely in ecclesial life (the balance fluctuating between conciliarity and primacy) will depend upon contingent historical factors and upon development under the guidance of the Holy Spirit' (Elucidation, sec. 8). On such a basis the Windsor Statement (1981) achieved a convergence of conflicting points of view, even though it could not fully resolve all of the problems which remain. It did, however, offer a doctrine of the papal primacy which many Anglicans could find acceptable. To say that the primacy of Rome has developed in the history of the Church through the guidance of the Spirit as a legitimate expression of universal oversight is to allow for a dynamic and developing ecclesiology that would modify both the absolute claim of the papacy to universal jurisdiction by divine right and the absolute claim of Rome that unity with the See of Peter is definitive of the Catholic Church. For those reasons many Anglicans, especially those in the Anglo-Catholic tradition, have found it possible to regard reunion with the Roman Catholic Church in a more hopeful way.

The response of the Sacred Congregation to the Venice and Windsor Statements, however, was negative and reasserted the absolute claims of the papacy, in particular that the papal primacy was provided for by Christ himself to the apostle Peter who 'received immediately and directly from Jesus Christ our Lord a true and proper primacy of jurisdiction'.[6] In addition it denied explicitly that the authority of papal jurisdiction and infallibility could be understood to have developed in response to human reason or historical need. Such authority, it claimed, is intrinsic to the successor of Peter and is constituent to the unity of the Catholic Church. Of course, many Roman Catholic theologians would reject the point of view held by the Sacred Congregation, but it does represent a significant point of view among Catholics − both Roman and Anglican − that the faith and practice of the Church is not subject to historical development but derives directly from the words and actions of Christ himself, and for that reason is unchanging in substance.

While the issue of the ordination of women is a vital one for many people in both communions, it does not have the theological significance of the claims of the papacy. It is, however, a very pointed illustration of the opposing points of view on the nature of development in the Church. On this issue many in the Anglo-Catholic tradition of Anglicanism have clearly sided with the position which is represented in the Roman Catholic Church by the Sacred Congregation. ARCIC raised the question of the ordination of women and recognized it as a new obstacle to reunion. It went on to say, however, that 'the principles upon which its doctrinal agreement rests are not affected by such ordinations; for it was concerned with the origin and nature of the ordained ministry and not with the question who can or cannot be ordained. Objections, however substantial, to the ordination of women are of a different kind from objections raised in the past against the validity of Anglican orders in general', (Elucidation, 1979, sec. 5). ARCIC was thus arguing for a point of view which many Anglicans and Roman Catholics would accept, namely, that the ordination of women can be seen as a legitimate development in the Church's understanding of the way in which the form of the ordained ministry is shaped by historical changes. There may be other objections to the ordination of women, but it is not, many would now think, contrary to the catholic understanding of the nature of the ordained ministry in the ministry of the Church.

The Sacred Congregation, however, took a very different position. It linked the question of eligibility for ordination to the nature of the sacrament of holy orders and cited the declaration *Inter Insigniores* of 1976 that the ordination of women cannot be allowed out of socio-cultural considerations because it is contrary to 'the "unbroken tradition throughout the history of the church, universal in the East and in the West" which must be "considered to conform to God's plan for his Church" ' ('Observations on the ARCIC Final Report', II, 3, note 2). Some Anglicans would agree with the point of view expressed by the Sacred Congregation because, on this issue at least, it reflects their understanding of the relation of the Church to historical change and development.

And here we can see just how complex the work for the unity of the Church can be. Reconciliation in faith and polity, even for those communions which have much in common, as do Anglicans and Roman Catholics, depends upon the doctrine of the Church and how the Church is understood to be the continuing presence of Christ in the world. Through their growing together both communions are being called to answer the same question: Is the Church to be understood in a static way, somehow transcendent of historical, cultural and social influences; or is the Church to be understood as a dynamic community, growing in its understanding of itself and its mission as it is guided into truth by the Spirit of Christ? As we have seen, the Oxford Movement, by regaining for Anglicanism a vision of the Church as the continuing presence of the incarnate Christ in the world, also faced that question. Many who called themselves Anglo-Catholics, however, held to a static ecclesiology; others, in the tradition of Maurice, Gore and Temple, argued for a more dynamic ecclesiology. The same question faces Anglo-Catholicism at the present time in its work towards unity, not only with the Roman Catholic Church but also with the churches of the Reformation.

It is certainly true that the relationship between Anglicans and the Roman Catholic Church has come a long way since Lord Halifax and the Abbé Portal dared to hope that the recognition of the validity of Anglican orders would lead to reunion with the Holy See. In that development Anglo-Catholicism has played a most decisive part by enabling the Anglican Communion to regain a heritage which had been lost or obscured. At the same time, however, in reaching out to the Roman Catholic Church, with which it has so much in common, the Anglican Communion cannot forget that it too is a product of the Reformation. The Tractarians often forgot or sought to explain away that part of their history. Anglo-Catholics today need to recall and, perhaps, relearn that they do claim to be a *reformed* Catholicism and that they must, therefore, take seriously what the Reformers on the Continent and those in England stood for in their protest against Rome. Anglo-Catholicism in the Anglican Communion can be of greatest service to future hopes of union with Rome only, I believe, as ways are found of reaching out also to those who are not Roman Catholics, but with whom Rome as well must some day be visibly united. To reach out to those other communities will not be a betrayal of the Oxford Movement. On the contrary, it will be to continue to learn what it means to believe that the Church is the incarnation of the exalted and risen Christ in the world.

5 Unity and the Churches of the Reformation

Much has been accomplished through conversations between Anglicans and the churches deriving from the Reformation. It has been of a quite different character from that which has been accomplished with Roman Catholicism because Anglicans do not so obviously share with many of the Protestant Churches a common ecclesiology and sacramental spirituality. The heritage of the Reformation is of another kind. Both, however, are essential for a vision of the universal Church of Christ — one which is truly catholic and apostolic.

Throughout the Anglican Communion there have been many movements towards unity with churches which, in one way or another, represent the tradition of the Reformation. Some, like the Church of South India, have been a result of missionary strategy when churches of various traditions have recognized the absurdity of maintaining divisions which have arisen out of essentially western conflicts. And there has, of course, been the very active involvement of the Anglican Communion in the World Council of Churches, which has created a major ecumenical force for Christians throughout the world as well as a growing awareness of the mission of the churches to social and economic problems. Here, however, I want to examine only two examples of ecumenical involvement, which are taking place in the United States. I am, of course, more familiar with them, but they also represent two patterns of ecumenical involvement which may help Anglican Churches in other places in their work towards visible unity with the non-episcopal churches. I am intentionally refraining from discussing what may well be even more important ecumenical movements between Anglicans and others in the Third World. Not only have I no personal knowledge of them, but also for me to do so from the perspective of Western ecumenical theology could result in serious 'theological imperialism'. The contribution of Anglicanism in the Third World to us in the West will probably be more radical than we can now imagine or anticipate.

There are several factors which make the ecumenical involvement of the Episcopal Church peculiar, although analogous situations exist elsewhere in the Anglican Communion. In the first place, it is required to deal not only with the historic churches of the Reformation or those which have grown out of other reform movements, but also with a variety of more recent churches which have come into existence as a result of particular circumstances in the diversity of American ecclesiastical history. It is, for example, involved with churches which have a strong racial or ethnic identity over and above their doctrinal and organizational stance. For many of these churches the Anglican heritage is not only foreign, but it can as well be reminiscent of past oppression and injustice. In addition, the Episcopal Church lives in a society which has a long tradition of pluralism and sectarianism and in which no one church – certainly not the Episcopal Church – can lay claim to having been institutionally or culturally identified with the nation's history. That creates a special problem. On the one hand, the Episcopal Church is a province of the worldwide Anglican Communion and shares in the catholic and apostolic heritage of Anglicanism. It cannot, therefore, simply regard itself as another denomination with no responsibility beyond that of its own internal organization. On the other hand, many other churches in the USA and, indeed, some Episcopalians themselves, do think of the Episcopal Church as another denomination – an odd one, perhaps, because of its more elaborate liturgy, its devotion to the episcopate, and its vague air of respectability – but not essentially different from other denominations.

In such a confused situation the Episcopal Church has engaged in two major ecumenical conversations with churches of the Protestant tradition: one with several of the Lutheran Churches in the United States — the Lutheran-Episcopal Dialogue (LED); the second with several other Protestant denominations — the Consultation on Church Union (COCU). In both, the particular involvement and witness of those who have inherited the tradition of the Oxford Movement have been especially significant. By being a constant reminder to the Episcopal Church of its heritage, Anglo-Catholicism has prevented the Church from moving too quickly into reunion with other churches in an unthinking response to American ecclesiastical pluralism. In a more positive way, Anglo-Catholicism has required the Episcopal Church and the others with whom it is involved to think more deeply about the nature of the Church and of the ministry in the Church. At the same time, such conversations have required Anglo-Catholics in their turn to see that the apostolic ministry involves something more than the possession of valid orders and the historic episcopate.

In September 1982, a major step towards reunion was taken by the Episcopal Church and some Lutheran Churches. (It is necessary to say 'some' Lutheran Churches because in the United States there is division within Lutheranism itself, as a result of historical factors in the development of Lutheranism there, as well as doctrinal differences. The American Lutheran Church, the Lutheran Church in America and the Association of Evangelical Lutheran Churches are uniting, and it is with them that the Episcopal Church has reached agreement. Some other Lutheran groups, especially the Missouri Synod, remain separated, although they have been involved in ecumenical discussions with the Episcopal Church.) The progress towards reunion was made possible because of the work done by the Anglican-Lutheran International Conversations which began in 1970 and the Lutheran-Episcopal Dialogue (LED) which began in the United States in 1969. Both have been very successful in discovering such a degree of consensus between the two traditions in doctrine and practice that each might recognize in the other a true communion in the Body of Christ. The Lutheran-Episcopal Dialogue has issued a series of reports and studies over a period of many years, most of which have now been published as *Lutheran-Episcopal Dialogue: Report and Recommendations*.[1] On the basis of the report and recommendations, a Resolution of the General Convention of the Episcopal Church (1982) stated that the Lutheran Churches and the Episcopal Church have been able to recognize one another as 'Churches in which the Gospel is preached' so that a 'relationship of Interim Sharing of the Eucharist' could be established between them. Because more theological work needs to be done on the nature of the apostolic ministry, the Resolution was careful to state that such an interim sharing does not yet signify a 'final recognition of each other's Eucharists or ministries', but it does acknowledge 'a mutual recognition of Eucharistic teaching sufficient for Interim Sharing of the Eucharist'. Such a step towards union has profound implications in many areas, not only in the United States but also in other provinces of the Anglican Communion as a whole. In the Lutheran–Episcopal Dialogue there are two matters which I believe to be of particular importance: first the nature of the doctrinal agreement which has been reached between two different traditions, and second the recognition that interim sharing in the eucharist may in itself be a way to greater unity.

LED followed a theological methodology very similar to the one used by ARCIC and ARC. Because of their long isolation from one another and the different historical circumstances in which each has developed, Lutheranism and Anglicanism have been shaped by different emphases in doctrine and spirituality and have developed different institutional structures for their common life. The theological conversations between the two churches show that doctrinal and historical differences can be resolved through a recognition that alternative ways of stating Christian belief and practice need not be a denial of unity in faith nor an ultimate barrier to unity in the eucharist. Rather, the traditions of both churches can be seen as authentic ways of preaching and teaching the same Gospel in continuity with the Apostolic Church. Thus LED has been able to issue Joint Statements on such fundamental doctrinal questions as justification, the gospel, eucharistic presence, the authority of scripture, and apostolicity. Each of these attempts to state what is essential in the Christian faith, while allowing for legitimate pluralism and diversity in formulation and recognizing the differences in emphasis which each tradition may give to a particular doctrine.

Given the different theological traditions and historical emphases of Lutheranism and Anglicanism, it was particularly significant that agreement could be reached on justification and apostolicity. The doctrine of justification, as I pointed out in chapter 1, is central to understanding of the gospel. Anglicans and Lutherans, however, have understood it in a different historical and theological context. For Lutherans the doctrine of justification is basic to their confessional statements in a way that it is not for Anglicans. The Joint Statement has been able to show that both emphases are necessary to a full understanding of the doctrine of justification. As the Joint Statement recognizes, the doctrine expresses the fundamental Christian belief that human beings in their sinfulness and alienation are accounted as righteous before God only for the merits and mediation of Jesus Christ. No human work can make us righteous. For Lutheranism that is the meaning of the gospel — the good news of our redemption in Christ — and in the history of Lutheranism it has led to the theological conviction that trust in God's faithfulness and mercy is the only hope of salvation. Human beings cannot save themselves; they depend upon a gracious and forgiving God.

Anglican theology would certainly not deny the doctrine of justification — even though Anglicans sometimes appear to do so in their preaching and practice! To deny it would be to deny the cross. But they have also seen in their history that justification in Christ involves sanctification in the Christian life through participation in the sacramental life of the Church. As we have seen, that is an emphasis which has developed in Anglican history from our understanding

80

of the Church as the continuation of the Incarnation and from a belief in our sacramental participation in Christ. By recognizing and accepting the value of both ways of talking about salvation, the two traditions will thus be able to complement one another. Anglicans through their relationship with Lutherans will be confronted more deeply with the centrality of the cross and the radical gift of grace. Their preaching and teaching about salvation frequently reflects a vague semi-pelagianism – that salvation can be won by good works and respectability – rather than the absolute demand placed upon human beings for trust in God's mercy. Lutherans, on the other hand, through their relationship with Anglicans, will be confronted more deeply with the appropriation of grace through the sacramental life of the Church – a calling to holiness of life lest justification lead, as Dietrich Bonhoeffer said, to 'cheap grace'.

In a similar way the Joint Statement on apostolicity was able to express the common view of both churches that the Church is apostolic in its foundation and that apostolicity includes succession in teaching, in the sacraments and in mission, as well as in an ordered and structured ministry of pastoral care and oversight (*episcope*). While many Lutheran Churches, for reasons arising out of historical circumstances, did not retain the historic episcopate as Anglicans have known it, and while many Anglicans would be unwilling to move towards full organic union with a church which does not have the historic episcopate, the two communions have been able to affirm that apostolicity has found different forms of expression in the Church's life and that those ways can be complementary and encouraging to one another rather than divisive and exclusive. In other words, in a way similar to the agreement which Anglicans have reached with Roman Catholics, the Lutheran–Episcopal dialogues have enabled the two churches to see in their own traditions that apostolic succession in the episcopate and apostolic succession in doctrine cannot be taken in isolation from one another: they are both essential to the fullness of apostolicity.

Once again the convergence of two traditions will be of

help to both. The Lutheran Churches affirm 'the full dignity of the pastoral office and are open to the historic episcopate as a valid and proper form of the office'.[2] They insist, however, that the historic episcopate must be seen to be in accord with the gospel, that is, 'in the context of faithful preaching of the Word and the right administration of the Sacraments'. The episcopate, as Anglicans have known it and as many Lutherans are coming to know it, can be an effective means of personal and sacramental focus for the apostolicity of the Church so long as it is not taken in isolation from the other forms of apostolic succession. From the Lutheran emphasis upon other forms of apostolic succession in the Church, Anglicans can learn that the apostolicity of the Church must also be expressed in doctrine and mission, and this can be of help to them in their conversations with other church traditions.

On the basis of the understanding which has been reached, LED, following a similar discussion of Lutheran orders between Lutherans and Roman Catholics, has called for a recognition that Lutheran orders are 'within the true succession of the Church and therefore merely defective in form or lacking fullness and not invalid'.[3]

The second area of importance to which conversations between Lutherans and Anglicans has led is the agreement on interim sharing of the eucharist, even though the ministries of the two communions have not been fully reconciled. Interim Eucharistic Fellowship with other churches was commended by the General Convention of the Episcopal Church in 1976, as a way towards unity through a common experience in worship. Certain provisions were laid down by the General Convention: that episcopal permission be obtained, that an approved form of prayer be used, that bread and wine should always be used, and that a priest of the Episcopal Church should always be a concelebrant. Under those terms Lutherans and Anglicans in the United States will now be able to join together in the common prayer and reception of the eucharist. To accept eucharistic sharing on the basis of fundamental agreement in faith, even while allowing for legitimate diversity in doctrine and ministry, expresses the conviction of both churches that the eucharist is not only a sign of the unity which Christians now have in Christ through their baptism but also a sign of a unity yet to be fulfilled. In baptism we are made one in Christ even though we are divided in our ecclesial life; in the eucharist 'we not only receive the strength to become what we are called to be, but also participate in the joys of the age to come when Christ shall be all in all'.[4]

That the eucharist can now be seen in this way represents a profound change in the thinking of many Anglicans and Lutherans, as well as many Roman Catholics. Certainly it represents a culmination for eucharistic teaching of those developments in ecclesiology which, as we have seen, began for Anglicans in the earlier part of this century. Anglican theology, through its continuing reflection upon the doctrine of the Incarnation, came to see the Church in terms of a catholicity yet to be realized, so that no one communion could be identified exclusively and uniquely with the one Church of Christ in its fullness. Since that time the rediscovery of some major themes in the New Testament, such as eschatology, has enabled us, and also required us, to see that the Church and all of its institutions, beliefs and practices stand under the judgement of the Kingdom which is yet to be, and that Christian people, by their baptism into the death and resurrection of Christ, live between the times, between the resurrection and the parousia. The Church, as the community of the baptized, is in pilgrimage, *in via*, towards the end of all things in God. Consequently, as many have come to believe, all churches ought to realise more deeply in their communal lives and in their relations with others the tentative nature of their beliefs and practices. The 'triumphalism' which in the past led some churches (both Protestant and Catholic) to claim that they possessed all the truth of the gospel can no longer be maintained against the witness of the New Testament to be absolute claim of the Kingdom of God.

A renewed awareness of the eschatological nature of the Church in the New Testament has had consequences for our understanding of the eucharist — that central act by which the Church proclaims and celebrates what it is and what it is yet to be. The eucharistic sharing we have with one another now is a sign and anticipation — partial and incomplete because of our sin and alienation — of the full unity which awaits the whole creation in the end when Christ, human and divine, is all in all. Because it is a sign and anticipation of a unity yet to be realized, the eucharist ought also to be seen as the way to a fullness of unity which we cannot now imagine, but for which we hope. The eucharist makes us one because it is the sacrament of the Incarnation, the unity of God and man in the Body of Christ; it is the incarnational sign of the end towards which we move in our pilgrimage, the final unity of the creation in God. In the catholic tradition the eucharist has rightly been called the medicine by which our sinful and broken souls are healed — Dr Pusey called the eucharist a 'comfort to the penitent'. It is to be hoped we are now coming to see that it is also the medicine by which the Church in all of its division can be healed. Eucharistic sharing may well be the most significant way in which all churches can discover their oneness in Christ who is the incarnate lord of the Church.

With Lutherans Anglicans share a great deal in doctrine and polity as well as in sacramental spirituality, even though their long separation from one another has obscured this communality. With many other churches deriving from the Reformation, however, the differences seem much greater. With those other churches also, with whom generally speaking Anglicans seem to share the least in their understanding of the Church and the sacramental life, ecumenical conversations of various kinds have been held throughout the world — the recent Covenant proposal in Britain is one example among many others. Just as it is not possible to speak of catholic unity without the involvement of the ancient churches of Rome and Orthodoxy, so also it is not possible to speak of catholic unity without the involvement of those Christians with whom Anglicans seem to share much less. Because of the variety of such conversations throughout the Anglican Communion, I shall here focus on that one with which I am most familiar. It is, I believe, representative of movements which are taking place elsewhere, even though it reflects the particular situation in the United States.

The Consultation on Church Union (COCU) began in 1961 when the Episcopal Church joined with several large Protestant denominations to seek a united church. In the course of years it has come to involve many other denominations, and this very diversity is itself significant and, perhaps, astounding to those unfamiliar with American ecclesiastical history. In addition to the Episcopal Church COCU includes: the African Methodist Episcopal Church, the African Methodist Episcopal Zion Church, the Christian Church (Disciples of Christ), the Christian Methodist Episcopal Church, the National Council of Community Churches, the Presbyterian Church in the United States, the United Church of Christ, the United Methodist Church, and the United Presbyterian Church in the USA. The diversity obviously reflects ethnic and cultural differences as well as theological ones. Since its beginning in 1961 COCU has led to co-operation in many pastoral and social areas, and it has produced a theological statement as a foundation for unity, *In Quest of a Church of Christ Uniting*, which has received a certain degree of acceptance among the various churches. The purpose and goal of COCU are quite clear, although they are as yet far from being realized. Its purpose is to bring about institutional and organizational unity and the mutual recognition of ministries and membership among all of the churches involved. Its goal is to create a new church which will be 'truly catholic, truly evangelical and truly reformed'.

The role of the Episcopal Church in COCU has been considerable, but not always clear. It is recognized by most Episcopalians concerned with the ecumenical movement that they must be involved with the mainstream of Protestant churches in the United States if for no other reason than that these are their neighbours and their brothers and sisters in Christ. In addition, the Episcopal Church has brought to the other churches in COCU an awareness of sacramental spirituality, of belonging to a worldwide communion, and of having a history and tradition which transcends local and national issues that are lacking in the experience of many of them. It would not be unfair to say that the doctrinal, liturgical and ministerial heritage of the Episcopal Church has to a considerable degree shaped the theological consensus which COCU has been able to achieve. And Episcopalians, in their turn, have of course learned much from the heritage of other churches in COCU and from the simple fact of having to examine their own tradition in order to present it in a positive way to others. Many of the things which Anglicans take for granted have had to be defended, justified and explained to those for whom they are foreign. Certainly, through conversations with those in the protestant and evangelical tradition Episcopalians have been shown aspects of the Gospel which they need to take more seriously than they sometimes do.

Following the kind of theological methodology which we have seen at work in other ecumenical conversations, the churches of COCU have reached a considerable degree of doctrinal consensus on all of the issues which were enunciated for Anglican ecumenical relations by the Chicago/Lambeth Quadrilateral, and there is even the hope that a future reconciliation of ministries can be achieved in order to make the mutual recognition of membership and ministries a possiblity. There have also been real achievements in worshipping and sharing together.

However, many in the Episcopal Church − especially those in the Anglo-Catholic tradition − have serious reservations about their involvement in COCU. Those reservations arise from two closely related concerns which have not been at issue in the discussions with Roman Catholics or Lutherans: they involve first the goal of COCU and second the vast differences which still exist, in spite of fundamental agreement on doctrine, between theological statements and the actual life of the Church.

The goal of COCU is to bring together many denominations into one united church which, as one of the COCU documents expressed it, will be 'a more inclusive expression of the oneness of the Church of Christ than any of the participating churches can suppose itself to be'. From all that we have discussed so far, it certainly can be said that such a goal is much to be hoped for. Gerald F. Moede, one of the most articulate spokesmen for COCU and a leading advocate of what has been called organic unity among the various churches, has written the following description of how he would envision this goal:

> Church union takes many different forms, and manifests itself in different ways. But inherent in each union is the desire that there be one visible manifestation of the catholic Church where previously there were several. All unions spring from the conviction that the unity among Christians for which Christ prayed was intended to be a unity in faith, worship and witness; that it should be, in fact, a unity which is not merely spiritually experienced by believers (important though that may be), but a manifest reality, apprehensible even by those who are not Christians at all.[5]

Dr Moede then analyses four areas in which the model of organic unity is important: faithfulness in mission, sacramental life (that is, both common worship and eucharistic sharing), corporate life and denominational identity. It is in the last two areas that many in the Episcopal Church appear to find the greatest difficulty with the goal of COCU and so have become reluctant to move ahead into a scheme of organic unity.

The goal of organic unity in the corporate life of the Church involves both church government and national organization. One of the most seriously held beliefs of those who argue for the COCU model of unity is that there should be an organic union of oversight in the one church, and that means one form of church government and only one focus of oversight in each place. Dr Moede asks:

If the bishop is the sacramental person standing at the point of intersection between the local eucharistic celebration and that of the universal Church, can ecumenical endeavor be satisfied with several bishops (or corporate episcopacies), organized under separate, autonomous, and even competing jurisdictions, claiming and exercising oversight of separated parts of the Christian fellowship in a particular place? This person answers 'No'.[6]

The goal of COCU is clearly one united church government, and, correlative with that, a united church government that will be, at least for the foreseeable future, organized on national lines. That is to say, COCU envisages a national church with a central government which may eventually establish a wider unity outside national borders, but one which also would have a national identity.

This goal creates serious problems for the Episcopal Church. First, Episcopalians fear the creation of an ecclesiastical organization which may provide bureaucratic unity but which will not overcome the deep-seated tendency of the Protestant churches in the United States towards denominationalism and sectarianism. Many indeed fear that governmental organization as COCU understands it will in fact produce a church that is just another denomination without a common identity. Second, there is strong resistance to the idea of national identity which is involved in the goal of COCU. While it is true that there have been national churches in other parts of the world which have risen above the limitations of nationalism, the dangers facing a new such church in the United States are many. We have already seen how one of the struggles in which the Oxford Movement engaged was to overcome the limitations which the national identity of the Established Church imposed upon the Church of England and to insist upon a vision of the Church which transcends national identity, even though it may be rooted in the history of a people. The Church of England itself, and many other churches in the Anglican Communion which resulted from colonial expansion, provide significant examples of the dangers that nationalism can produce. While it is true that a church must be the Church in a particular place, and thus an incarnational presence of Christ, it is also true that it cannot be limited by its location in that place. Episcopalians, who know something of an international identity and communion as well as denominationalism, do fear the possibility of nationalism, no matter how carefully defined.

But the goal of COCU raises a much larger concern. One of the persistent themes of the ecumenical movement, especially through the development of the World Council of Churches, has been that denominational identity must undergo significant transformation in a united church. The New Delhi statement on unity in 1961 expresses this conviction well: 'The achievement of unity will involve nothing less than a death and rebirth of many forms of church life as we have known them. We believe that nothing less costly can finally suffice.'[7] Certainly all thoughtful people ought to agree with this, for it is the call to end denominationalism. The Episcopal Church, however, even while granting the truth of the principle, is seriously concerned about the consequences which may result from the ecumenical situation in the USA. Their concern arises not simply from a fear that it might lose some of its customs and practices in a united church, but the belief that the fundamental differences in ecclesiology and sacramental spirituality which exist in the various churches need to be more fully expressed and worked through. As many people have observed, there is a considerable difference between what is accomplished in ecumenical dialogue by theologians and ecumenists and the way in which a particular church lives out its life in ministry, word and sacrament. That difference is especially important for the way in which the ordained ministry is understood to function in the community. In the Episcopal Church (as in Anglican Churches elsewhere) there is a long history of living with the episcopate as an office which is chiefly pastoral and sacramental and a focus of unity not only with other provinces of the Anglican Communion, but also with the

Universal Church. While at times the administrative aspect of the episcopate seems to overwhelm those other aspects, nonetheless the Anglican heritage is to *want* a bishop to be a chief pastor and sacramental focus for the Church. For many of the churches involved in COCU, who might be willing to accept the historic episcopate as the best and most ancient form of church government, there has been no such heritage. Church officials, above the level of those who have immediate pastoral care, are more often perceived as the administrative arm of a church. Reconciliation of ministries will not therefore immediately accomplish a reconciliation of the ways in which the hierarchical structure of the ministry is perceived in the life of a church. Reconciliation of ministries, in other words, involves more than conferring valid orders on the ministry of another church or a mutual recognition of the validity of orders among the churches. Anglicans have learned and are learning through all of their ecumenical conversations that the historic episcopate is one important aspect of the apostolic and catholic character of the Church, but at a deeper level what is involved is an ethos, hard to define but no less real, involving many strands and configurations through which the distinctive nature of Anglicanism is expressed.

Certainly these reservations do not lead to the conclusion that the Episcopal Church ought to withdraw from COCU nor that Anglicans elsewhere should retreat from conversations leading towards unity with other non-episcopal churches. They only suggest that it is not yet clear what the future shape of church unity may be and that it will take many years of living together for us all to come to a common understanding of what it is truly to be catholic and apostolic, not only in ministerial structure and doctrinal consensus, but also in the way in which important elements in the Church are expressed in the life of Christian people.

In this ecumenical situation, as in others elsewhere, those who are the inheritors of the Oxford Movement at the end of the twentieth century may well be facing the same challenge that faced Gore and others at the end of the nineteenth: if Anglo-Catholicism is not always to be on the defensive in the face of movements which it sees as dangerous to its catholic and apostolic heritage, what is now the positive contribution it can make to the unity of the Church in the twenty-first century?

NOTE

In 1978 the Episcopal Church undertook a major theological evaluation of the various ecumenical conversations in which it is engaged. The Detroit Report, as it was called, and other studies and reports were published in a volume which I have used extensively in this chapter — *A Communion of Communions: One Eucharistic Fellowship*. In the course of the evaluation the theologians and ecumenical consultants who were involved thought it important to state once again on what basis the Episcopal Church, as a province of the Anglican Communion, could reach doctrinal consensus with other traditions. The Chicago/Lambeth Quadrilateral, it was believed, needed elaboration and development in consideration of the new issues which have arisen during many decades of ecumenical involvement since the Quadrilateral was proposed in 1888. Although it does not have official endorsement, I cite the statement on principles of unity, as an important (although not well known) example of ecumenical theology:

We affirm as principles on which our own unity is established, and we propose as our principles for unity with other churches:

1. A mutual recognition that the Holy Scriptures of the Old and New Testament are the word of God as they witness to God's action in Jesus Christ and the continuing presence of His Spirit in the Church. They are the authoritative norm for catholic faith in Jesus Christ and for the doctrinal tradition of the Gospel. Therefore we can declare that they contain all things necessary for salvation.

2. A mutual recognition that the Ancient Creeds are the form through which the Christian

91

Church, early in its history in the world, understood, interpreted, and expressed its faith in the Triune God. The continuing doctrinal tradition is the form through which the Church seeks to understand, interpret, and express its faith in continuity with the Ancient Creeds and in its awareness of the world to which the Word of God must be preached.

3. A mutual recognition that the Church is the sacrament of God's presence to the world and the sign of the Kingdom for which we hope. The presence and hope are made active and real in the Church and in Christian men and women through the preaching of the Word of God, through the Gospel sacraments of Baptism and Eucharist, and through our apostolate to the world in order that it may become the Kingdom of our God and of his Christ.

4. A mutual recognition that apostolicity is evidenced in continuity with the teaching, the ministry, and the mission of the apostles. Apostolic *teaching* must be founded upon the Holy Scriptures and the ancient fathers and creeds, drawing its proclamation of Jesus Christ, and His Gospel for each new age from these sources, not merely reproducing them in a transmission of verbal identity. Apostolic *ministry* exists to promote, safeguard, and serve apostolic teaching. All Christians are called into this ministry by their Baptism. In order to serve, lead, and enable this ministry, some are set apart and ordained in the historic orders of Bishop, Presbyter, and Deacon. We understand the historic episcopate as central to this apostolic ministry and to the reunion of Christendom. Apostolic *mission* is itself a

succession of apostolic teaching and ministry inherited from the past and carried into the present and future. Bishops in apostolic succession are, therefore, the focus and personal symbols of this inheritance and mission as they preach and teach the Gospel and summon the people of God to their mission of worship and service.[8]

6 The Future of the Oxford Movement

This study of the Oxford Movement and its consequences for Anglicanism began with a discussion of the doctrine of the Incarnation and how that doctrine has affected our understanding of the relationship between Christ and the Church. We have seen how the doctrine, but even more the event which the doctrine attempts to define, was a central focus for the Tractarians, enabling them to regain a vision of the Church as a divinely established and commissioned community in the world; and we have seen how it has enabled subsequent generations to explore the calling of Anglicanism in the larger community of the Christian Church. The belief that God trusts us with himself, that he commits himself to us and to our history in the life of Jesus, and that he continues to trust us with himself in the life of the Church, has had profound consequences for the way in which Anglicans have come to understand the Church and themselves. In this final chapter I want to return to the theme of the Incarnation and ask how an incarnational theology may give a new sense of vision to Anglo-Catholicism as the Anglican Communion faces many new challenges in the future. My belief is that the responsibility facing those who would still call themselves Anglo-Catholics and inheritors of the Oxford Movement is to continue to witness to the mystery of the Incarnation and to discover how that witness can be of great importance in the complex and difficult ecumenical calling of the Anglican Communion.

In order to explain that belief I want to write somewhat more personally than I have done in previous chapters about Anglo-Catholicism itself. The term 'Anglo-Catholic' is no longer as widely used by Anglicans in the catholic tradition as it once was — at least not in the United States. For many it has become associated with rigidity in doctrine, a negative approach to new developments in the Church, and a fussy ritualism and piety. And yet, from the history of Anglo-Catholicism I hope we have been able to see that it is, in fact, a term which ought to have a very different significance. The catholic movement has contributed much to the way in which Anglicans understand themselves, and its witness has been of great importance in many areas of the Church's life of worship and mission. I want, therefore, to say something about my reasons for considering myself still an Anglo-Catholic and about my hopes for the future of Anglo-Catholicism. I want to do that not simply as personal testimony (to which the American religious tradition may be somewhat excessively prone), but in the hope that my reasons and hopes may help others to see for themselves something of the calling of the catholic movement in the Church at large. How people identify themselves within the broad spectrum of religious commitment comes about for a variety of personal reasons, but if we can share with others our reasons for believing as we do, perhaps we can discover more about ourselves and much more about the mystery of Christ and his Church.

I am a Christian because I believe in the Incarnation of God in Christ. There are, of course, many reasons for believing in the Incarnation, just as there are many ways of stating what that event was and continues to be. And all Christians who confess belief in the event of the Incarnation must find for themselves what it means in their lives and how it enables them to enter more deeply into the Gospel of salvation which it expresses. As I have reflected upon my belief in the Incarnation in thought, prayer, worship and action, I have come to see that it is the definitive and historic expression of the mystery which I believe to be at the heart of reality — that mystery which calls me and all human beings beyond our sins and failures into the fullness of our common humanity. That mystery I would call the trust by which we are able to give and receive gifts. It is, of course, the mystery for which we use the name 'God'. I like to think of it as the trust to give and receive gifts because all human beings know something about gifts. We know the gift of life itself, both as we have received it and have given it. We know also the gift of love which we share with one another, most clearly when we learn that love is always a gift freely given and not something to which we can lay claim by right of possession. To learn that we live by gift and by the giving of gifts to others is to enter most fully into our humanity because it is to learn what it is to trust not only other human beings but to trust reality itself. Giving and receiving gifts can take many forms, from a simple act of generosity to the most profound sharing of life with another person. In every case, however, it involves trust: on the one hand, that what is given will be accepted; and on the other, that the one who gives to us is to be trusted. To live by gift is to trust: that is one way to talk about the mystery at the heart of reality for which we use the name 'God'.

As a Christian I believe the event of the Incarnation to be the full and perfect expression in human history of that mystery of gift and trust. It is the personal expression of the gift to us of the eternal and divine reality of God in the life of the man Jesus of Nazareth, and it exemplifies the trust of the God who gives himself to us without reservation by entering into our history as the gift of himself. And it is also the expression of the gift of ourselves which in the human life of Jesus we, by the Spirit, can give in trust to the One who creates, redeems and sanctifies us. The mystery of the Incarnation is that the gift given to us in Jesus Christ enables us to give the gift of ourselves to others and to God and to trust in him who trusts us with himself. The gift given to us and the gift of ourselves which we can offer are one in Jesus Christ, true God and true man, as Christian faith has always confessed. To be in the Christian community, to have communion with God in Christ, to know the indwelling presence of the Spirit, to share in the life of prayer, and to love and serve others — all of that, and much more, is to live in trust by the one gift, Jesus Christ, the meeting together of God and man. Believing that makes me a Christian, no matter how difficult being a Christian may sometimes be.

Other Christians would, doubtless, express the substance of their belief in different ways and, consequently, live out what they believe in other ecclesial traditions. I, however, am an Anglican, and in particular an Anglo-Catholic, because I have found in the catholic tradition of Anglicanism a way of being, believing and acting which, by grace, enables me to trust in the giver of the gift and so to trust that the gift of myself will be received and transformed, no matter how limited and distorted by sin my life may be. I say that not because the Anglican Church has a monopoly on truth, nor because it can never err or be disobedient to the Gospel, nor because it is always pure in doctrine and polity, but because I have found the sacramental life in Anglicanism to be the personal and communal expression of what I believe to be true about the Incarnation and, consequently, true about the nature of reality itself.

The revival of the sacramental life in Anglicanism began with the Oxford Movement, and it has ever since characterized Anglo-Catholicism. Some in the Anglo-Catholic tradition have seen the sacramental life of the Church in a juridical and even static way – as a legal and moral obligation to do what is commanded. For others, however, it has led to the development of a spirituality through which we have come to believe that to live a life centred upon the sacraments is to learn to live through the gift of grace and through trust in the giver of the gift. A sacramental spirituality is a way of life in which we know the ambiguity, sin and disorder which affects all human beings and even the Church itself, and yet it enables us to trust that in our disorder and confusion God's grace is given to us. To believe in the sacramental presence of Christ is to believe that we live by gift and in the trust that the eternal God comes into our lives and is accomplishing his purpose in us and in the Church. For the Tractarians the eucharist was the action of the Church which most deeply expressed and made real the event of the Incarnation, and those who have

97

come after them have always insisted that the eucharist should be the principal action of the people of God as they are gathered for worship. Whatever the failures and distortions to which Anglo-Catholicism has been prone, its greatest gift and strength has been its continuing witness to a sacramental spirituality as a way of living out the mystery of God made man, the mystery of trust in the One who gives himself to us in the gifts which we give to him.

Such a spirituality ought to help those who continue in the heritage of the Oxford Movement to come to a renewed sense of our future witness in Anglicanism. It is a witness which will continue to arise out of that form of incarnational and sacramental theology which I have attempted to define as central to our history, if we are able to discern between those issues and causes in our past which may not now be as important as we once thought they were and those new issues and causes into which the Church is being led by the Spirit of Christ. The Anglican Communion is now faced with many perplexities, ambiguities and crises. Some of them, as I have suggested in earlier chapters, are a result of our particular ecumenical calling; others are a result of the serious questions which face all Christian people in this century: political and economic change, the environment, the threat of nuclear holocaust, and many others. It is obvious that Anglicanism cannot by itself provide any answers to the crises facing all human beings, any more than Anglo-Catholicism can provide the answers to the particular problems facing the Anglican Communion. In such situations we do what we can in response to the call on us, in trust that whatever gifts we have to offer to others will be received. It is clear to me, and I believe to many others, that the gift which Anglicanism has to give is in the work for reunion of the Church, the visible unity of the Body of Christ. Our hope is that the one Church of Christ may be the community through which we human beings can find our way in the crises which face us all. If that should be the case, then we who are Anglo-Catholics must ask ourselves what gifts we have to bring and to receive in the ecumenical calling of the Anglican Communion. What have we learned in our history as a people who witness to the Incarnation through a sacramental spirituality?

One of the most notable characteristics of Anglicanism (and often its most vexing characteristic to those in other churches) is that we find it very difficult to define ourselves as a church in a very precise way. We cannot define ourselves in terms of a central jurisdiction (neither Lambeth nor Canterbury functions in that way) and an infallible teaching office as Roman Catholics claim to be able to do, nor can we define ourselves in terms of a confessional stance as many in the reformed tradition do. At one time, it was possible to claim for Anglicanism a linguistic and cultural unity, but because of the rapid growth of the Anglican Communion outside the English-speaking world and our greater sense of a catholicity which is neither national nor cultural, this is no longer true. Nevertheless, we do seem to have a sense of what it is to be an Anglican and not something else. With all of our diversity we can recognize one another.

Our sense of unity and identity derives, I believe, from the particular way in which the mystery of the Incarnation has been lived out in our history. It is from our way of living out the implications of an incarnational theology that we can discern some of the gifts we have to offer to the larger Christian community. On the basis of our participation in a variety of ecumenical conversations I believe we can see those gifts in three areas: 1 our sense of the Church in history which gives us a particular understanding of authority; 2 our sense of continuity with the past and with the universal Church; and 3 our sense of a catholicity yet to be realized. Each of those gifts has arisen within Anglicanism as a consequence of what began with the Oxford Movement, and each ought to be now the particular witness of Anglo-Catholicism within Anglicanism and the larger Christian community.

1 The nature of authority in the Church was one of the most vexing questions for the early leaders of the Oxford Movement. On the one hand, they felt called to resist the

99

authority of the State in church affairs and to assert the divine commission of the Church in society. On the other hand, many of the Tractarians and their successors felt it equally necessary to oppose the authoritarian and absolutist claims of Rome. As we have seen, the need to define the nature of authority led initially to a somewhat a-historical elevation of the authority of the Fathers and to an equally a-historical doctrine of apostolic succession in the episcopate. Neither of those ways proved to be viable, although each contained much truth. By the end of the nineteenth century there began to emerge what I have called an incarnational theology and sacramental spirituality in which lay an acknowledgement that the authority of Christ could be, and had been, mediated in history through fallible and sinful human beings. That sense of authority, as it has continued to develop in Anglicanism, is nebulous and indefinite, at times frustrating in its lack of clarity and precision to those who ask for a more precise doctrine, but it is an attempt to live out something of great importance about Jesus Christ in the Christian faith, namely, that the Church in history is both divine and human, transcendent of space and time yet deeply enmeshed in the shifts and changes of human affairs, holy and without spot or blemish yet composed of sinful, fallible and confused human beings. It is to confess that the Church, in all of its ambiguity and confusion, is one with Christ, who is himself the active and personal presence of the eternal God in the ambiguities and confusions of that human history to which God has given himself in trust. For such a theological point of view, the Church is that community to which God has given himself for the working out of his will and purpose in the world.

There are many ways in which the authority of Christ is mediated to us, and, through our ecumenical conversations with other traditions, we, as Anglicans, have begun to discover both the diversity and the richness of ways other than our own. The gift which we have to give is not really a particular doctrine about the forms and institutions through which authority is mediated to us, for many of the ways which are a part of our heritage − the ministry, scripture, tradition, human reason and the charismatic prophet – we share with others in varying degrees. Rather it is a fundamental attitude towards the Catholic and Apostolic Church, with all of its weakness and fallibility, as the continuing presence of the incarnate lord. Anglicanism through its history has learned and continues to learn that the Incarnation shows us that the authority of Christ for us and for his Church is something which we shall never grasp fully nor express in a totally adequate way: we perceive that authority through the many diverse, at times conflicting, ways in which the Church and Christian people have witnessed to Christ in every generation through doctrine, ecclesiastical institutions, forms of worship and moral action. Through all the diversity, however, there remains the conviction that the Church has a divine commission and calling to be lived out in history. In other words, the Church, in which we come to know the authority of Christ, is the sacrament of Christ: his real presence in the materiality of our lives. Such a way of thinking ought to help us to see that the Church is called into a pilgrimage of trust in the God who has given himself in history, so that whatever security we may have derives ultimately from his gift.

Such a way is not always easy, for human beings do want security in religious matters as well as in others. And many in the Anglo-Catholic tradition have found they could not follow that way and have sought greater assurance in other religious traditions. But Dr Pusey, despite his intransigence in certain areas, did follow it, as have many others, and it is a heritage which the Oxford Movement has given to us: to be a community of faith which rests only upon the certainty that God was and continues to be in Christ, reconciling the world to himself and bringing his Church into the fullness of his Kingdom. Dr Pusey once explained the difference between himself and Cardinal Newman by saying that Newman trusted in bishops whereas he trusted in the Church. And he continued to do that through all of the controversies of his later life and even the scorn which he suffered. Dr Pusey saw that to trust in the Catholic Church is ultimately to trust in the mystery of the Incarnation and in the sacramental presence of Christ in his Church — even during the difficult years for the Church of England. That sense of authority is a gift which those who stand in his tradition ought to be able to share with others.

2   The Church, however, is incarnational and sacramental, and for that reason its institutions are important and even essential to its life. That too is one of our legacies from the Oxford Movement and another of the gifts which, through our history, we have to give to others. The Oxford Movement enabled Anglicans to believe that with all their fallibility and limitedness, the institutional structures of the Church, most especially the ordained ministry, have a divine foundation and calling. They are the form through which Christ is present as the Church lives out its mission in history. We have seen how the historic episcopate has become for us that form of ministry which is of paramount importance. It is the institution which has, more than any other, enabled us to maintain our identity in different historical and cultural situations and to have a sense of unity, not only among ourselves, but with the Catholic and Apostolic Church. While we have from time to time romanticized the historic episcopate, taking it in isolation from the larger meaning of apostolicity (which has had unhappy consequences for our relations with other churches), nonetheless it has continued to be for us a central focus of an incarnational and sacramental understanding of the Church in history. Our responsibility now, as those to whom the gift of the historic episcopate has been given, is to discover how we can give it as a gift to others, making it neither a burden nor an imposition.

It is not my hope here to resolve those many vexed questions about the historic episcopate which have troubled Anglicans for centuries and are now troubling others. In the final analysis I am not certain we shall ever resolve, for example, the question whether the episcopate is of the *esse* (essence), *bene esse* (well-being) or *plene esse* (fullness) of the Church. The answer will depend upon the context within which the question is asked, and so will never satisfy everyone. I do want to suggest, however, that the historic episcopate is essential for the way in which we have come to understand ourselves as a sacramental and incarnational community within the Catholic Church.

What we and other traditions now see more clearly than, perhaps, we saw in the past is that the ministry of the Catholic Church is the ministry of Christ in his Church. In the course of its development from the New Testament to the present, the ministry of the Church has taken on different shapes and certain aspects have sometimes been emphasized to the exclusion of others of equal importance. But always the ministry which Christian people, whether lay or ordained, exercise is the ministry of Christ himself. From this flow two important consequences: the ministry is personal, by which we mean that the ministry of Christ is exercised through human beings; and it is the expression of Christ's pastoral care for his people, by which we mean that it is the continuity of the Church with its foundation in Christ and with its future in the fullness of Christ, the one who is the eternal high priest and shepherd of all people. In other words, the ministry, however it may be exercised, is the sacramental presence of Christ in the life of the Church, and it is, therefore, the continuation of his ministry in the Incarnation. The ministry is the visible sign of the trust in which God gives himself to the Church, and it is the visible sign of the gift which human beings make of themselves to do God's work in the world. In Christ both signs are one.

In these days there is much confusion and no little change in the way in which Christians of all traditions understand the ministry. Quite rightly, I believe, we have come to see the ministry of the Church as the vocation of all Christian people, not as something limited to those who are ordained. But that new awareness (or actually rediscovery of something much older) and many other factors have created problems for our understanding of the ordained ministry itself. In many churches serious questioning is taking place about the nature, function and authority of those who have been ordained. We can see such questioning in the issues of clerical celibacy, the ordination of women, the rejection of priestly authority in an increasingly secular society and the new role of lay people in positions of authority. Certainly there are no easy answers to the questions posed to us by those developments. As it has with similar questions in the past, the Church must live with them and trust that it will be led by the Spirit into a resolution of some of its dilemmas and difficulties. But, in that process, to see the ministry as the personal and sacramental presence of Christ and as the continuation of his pastoral care can be of great importance. It is here that the historical experience of Anglicanism, especially in the catholic tradition, can be especially helpful.

With all of its faults and limitations and with all of the corruptions and arrogance to which bad bishops have been prone, the episcopate has become for Anglicans a human and personal focus of what the ministry is and ought to be. It has functioned for us as a sacramental sign of Christ's ministry in the Incarnation and of the historic continuity of that ministry in human beings. In other words, the historic episcopate has come to express for us the pastoral care of Christ through apostolic succession. And that, perhaps, would suggest that it was not totally wrong for Newman to trust in bishops, even though he thought they failed him. A bishop has many functions to perform, but he is first and last the pastor of God's people in a particular place and time. In his pastoral oversight all other forms of ministry find their focus because he stands in continuity with the apostles whom Christ charged to preach the Gospel and to feed his sheep.

However confused their vision was at times, the Tractarians were trying to see the historic episcopate in such a way. In all of the Tracts bishops are spoken of as successors of the apostles because they have a divine commission to minister in the world as Christ; they were not just officers of state or ecclesiastical dignitaries who could be done away with when they became redundant. The subsequent theological work of those in the catholic tradition of Anglicanism as well as in other Christian communities may have clarified and broadened our conception of the apostolic ministry, removing from it certain accretions and limitations, but the fundamental insight of the Tractarians remains for us a gift which we ought to give to the Church of Christ.

3 One of the most characteristic claims of Anglo-Catholicism has been that the Anglican Church, in all its diversity, is truly a part of the Catholic and Apostolic Church, and its chief goal has been to re-call Anglicanism to its heritage. For Anglo-Catholics both the claim and the goal have sometimes meant living with many anomalies and inconsistencies. Some Anglo-Catholics can still remember the battles that were fought, the victories gained and the defeats suffered in the struggle with 'low-church' bishops, priests and lay people. Too often the claim and the goal found expression only in externals, but more often they represented a struggle to incarnate in Anglicanism a vision of catholicity which could and did transform the Anglican Communion. Much of that is past history, for many of the old battles seem irrelevant to the different situation now facing the Anglican Church in all parts of the world. But the claim and goal are still very real, even though the issues have changed. Anglo-Catholicism is still a movement within the Anglican Church which witnesses to catholicity. Of the many new issues which now call for that witness, the role of Anglo-Catholics in the ecumenical movement is, I believe, one of the most important. The ecumenical movement and our place in it cuts deeply into our claim to catholicity; it exposes our weakness and it can show us our strength.

By its very claim to be a part of the Catholic and Apostolic Church Anglicanism knows itself to be incomplete. In a society where increasingly the supports of national and cultural identity are being taken away, where we are discovering our smallness and insignificance both ecclesiastically and politically, we are being required to ask ourselves what it means to live with fragmentation and separation from other Christian traditions. Whatever some of our pretensions may have been in the past, we know that we cannot define 'Catholicism' in terms of ourselves — the Anglican Church does not set the limits and boundaries of the Catholic Church. What we have come to see, however, is that we can witness to a certain form of catholicity in the larger Christian community: we have gifts to give to others which we have learned through our own history; but to give these gifts to others is not enough: belief in the Incarnation requires of us that we be able also to receive the gifts which others have to offer us.

In an ecumenical age it can be a platitude to say that we ought to be open to receive the gifts which other Christian traditions have to offer us. Such a statement can be seen simply as a courteous and broad-minded attitude towards our 'separated brethren'. But for a community for which the event of the Incarnation has been a major paradigm of the Church such a statement must be taken more seriously. Our desire for the visible unity of the Church and our work towards that hope ought to arise much more out of an awareness that we are a community of people who, in our incompleteness, need the gifts of others for the fullness of catholicity. To believe in the Church as the sacramental presence of the incarnate Christ means that only as we receive the gifts of others can we offer the gifts of our tradition. The gifts which other traditions offer to us and which we offer are one gift in Christ. The Incarnation of God in Christ makes the giving and receiving of gifts possible: that is the only foundation for the unity of the Church.

The way to the reunion of the Church will be long and difficult, and the vision of what reunion may mean for all churches is still obscure. It is a hope offered in Christ – a final fulfilment yet to be revealed. But along the way Anglo-Catholicism has its work to do. The Incarnation is the personal sign of God's trust in committing himself to us and a personal sign of our trust in committing ourselves to God. As we have seen, Anglo-Catholics have in a variety of ways sought to witness to that mutual trust. This has often entailed a willingness to live with fragmentation, diversity and incompleteness because we have believed that God is working out his purpose in his world, in the Church and in us, directing all things to their fullness in Christ. In the past that witness has not always been easy, and in the future it is likely to be even more difficult. But belief in the Incarnation ought to enable us to live and work in the trust that God in Christ by the power of the Spirit is calling the Church to a future which we cannot yet see, but which we can believe to be the fullness of Christ in his Church.

The Anglican Church is only one small part of the Catholic Church; without others who also believe in Christ it is incomplete, as, indeed, all other churches are incomplete without one another. Perhaps one of the most important gifts which Anglicanism has to offer is its sense of being Catholic and yet being incomplete. Anglo-Catholics, who have for so many years witnessed to the catholicity of Anglicanism, may now be called to witness to our need for the gifts which others — Roman Catholics, Orthodox, Lutherans, evangelical Protestants, and all the rest of the divided Body of Christ — have to give to us. What those gifts may be, only others can show us out of their tradition and present life. That we should recognize and, indeed, give thanks for our need may well be our calling. To live by gift is to believe in the Incarnation. In the giving and receiving of gifts we can come to a deeper trust in the one gift who makes all other gifts possible, Jesus Christ, the Father's gift to us and our gift to the Father.

My hope for Anglo-Catholicism is then neither a concrete plan nor a definite programme. My hope is, quite simply, that we shall, even more than in the past, learn what it is to live by gift: to claim nothing for ourselves except the one thing which we have learned and are learning by believing that God is in Christ, reconciling the world to himself. To learn that is to learn what it is we have to give and what it is we have to receive, and so to learn what it is to trust in the God who is, in Christ, working out his purpose, even in the anomalies and oddities of the Anglican Communion.

Notes

CHAPTER 1   Christ and the Church: the Heritage of the Oxford Movement

1   Oxford and New York, 1979.
2   For a serious theological and political analysis of *Christianity and the World Order*, see the collection of lectures edited by Kenneth Leech, *Christianity Reinterpreted? A Critical Examination of the 1978 Reith Lectures* (Penarth, South Glamorgan, 1979). The lectures by Eric Mascall and Kenneth Leech are especially helpful for their theological criticism of Dr Norman.
3   Norman, *Christianity and the World Order*, p. 77.
4   John Hick (ed.) (London and Philadelphia, 1977).
5   The most thorough analysis and criticism of the points of view developed in *The Myth of God Incarnate* are to be found in Michael Goulder (ed.) *Incarnation and Myth: The Debate Continued*. There are several collections of constructive essays, the most interesting of which, I believe, are: A. E. Harvey (ed.), *God Incarnate: Story and Belief* (London, 1981) and Durstan R. McDonald (ed.), *The Myth/Truth of God Incarnate* (Wilton, Conn., 1979).
6   From *The Book of Common Prayer* of the Episcopal Church in the USA (New York, 1979), p. 864.
7   The quotation can be found in J. N. D. Kelly, *Early Christian Doctrines*, revised edn (New York, 1978), p. 352.
8   Richard Hooker, *The Laws of Ecclesiastical Polity*, Book V, lvi, 13. There are various editions of Hooker's *Laws*. A new critical edition is forthcoming in the United States: *The Folger Library Edition of the Works of Richard Hooker*, general editor W. Speed Hill (Belknap Press of the Harvard University Press).

CHAPTER 2   The Oxford Movement: a Vision Regained

1 F. Oakeley, 'Sacramental Confession', *British Critic*, 33 (no. 66) (1843), p. 314. The quotation is cited in the very fine study by Alf Härdelin, *The Tractarian Understanding of the Eucharist* (Uppsala, 1965), p. 83.
2 See Härdelin, *Tractarian Understanding*, p. 84. Wilberforce's study, *The Doctrine of the Incarnation of Our Lord Jesus Christ, in its Relation to Mankind and to the Church*, 3rd edn (London, 1850), is of major importance in the development of Anglican incarnational theology.
3 See Louis Weil, *Sacraments and Liturgy: The Outward Signs* (Oxford, 1983).

CHAPTER 3   The Anglican Church: Catholic and Apostolic

1 London, 1958, preface to the first edition, p. xxviii.
2 N. P. Williams, 'The Theology of The Catholic Revival', in N. P. Williams and C. Harris (eds), *Northern Catholicism* (London, 1933), p. 220.
3 London, 1946, p. 187.
4 This and other major statements, pertaining to ecumenical relations, made by the Episcopal Church in the United States and Lambeth Conferences can be found in J. Robert Wright (ed.), *A Communion of Communions: One Eucharistic Fellowship* (New York, 1979). The quotation appears on p. 258.
5 *A Communion of Communions*, pp. 260–1.

CHAPTER 4   Unity and the Roman Catholic Church

1 Published in *Documents on Anglican-Roman Catholic Relations I/II*, United States Catholic Conference (Washington, 1972), pp. 101–5.
2 Reprinted in the *Final Report* (London, 1982), pp. 108–16.
3 *Documents*, p. 105.
4 *The Final Report*, the Canterbury Statement, section 4. All subsequent references to the ARCIC Statements are to the *Final Report*.

5 'Observations on the ARCIC Final Report', II, 2, originally printed in *Origins*, 6 May 1982, vol. 11, no. 47, pp. 752–6; reprinted in *Ecumenical Bulletin*, July–August 1982, no. 54, pp. 15–18.

6 'Observations', III, 1, quoting the Constitution, *Pastor Aeternus*, chapter 2, of Vatican Council I.

CHAPTER 5   Unity and the Churches of the Reformation

1 Forward Movement Publication (Cincinnati, 1981). The report contains the LED Dialogues, Series II, and other relevant material. All subsequent references to LED documents are taken from this volume.

2 LED, 'Joint Statement on Apostolicity', III, 5.

3 LED, III, 5.

4 LED, 'Joint Statement on Eucharistic Presence', 6.

5 Gerald F. Moede, 'All in Each Place One: The Consultation on Church Union' in *A Communion of Communions*, p. 148.

6 Ibid., p. 154.

7 Cited in ibid., p. 159, from W. Visser't Hooft (ed.), *The New Delhi Report* (London, 1962), p. 117.

8 *A Communion of Communions*, pp. 16, 17.

Further Reading

In addition to the books and documents to which I have referred in the notes, the following would be helpful for reading in particular areas. Unfortunately, some are no longer in print, but most libraries should have them or be able to find them.

Historical studies

Henry R. T. Brandreth, *The Oecumenical Ideals of the Oxford Movement* (London, 1947).

Yngve Torgny Brilioth, *The Anglican Revival: Studies in the Oxford Movement* (London and New York, 1925).

James Carpenter, *Gore: A Study in Liberal Catholic Thought* (London, 1960).

Owen Chadwick (ed.), *The Mind of the Oxford Movement* (Stanford, Calif., 1960).

A. M. Ramsey, *F. D. Maurice and the Conflicts of Modern Theology* (Cambridge, 1951).

A. M. Ramsey, *From Gore to Temple* (London, 1960); USA edn: *An Era in Anglican Theology* (New York, 1960).

Bernard M. G. Reardon, *From Coleridge to Gore* (London, 1971).

George Tavard, *The Quest for Catholicity: A Study in Anglicanism* (London, 1964).

Lionel S. Thornton, *Richard Hooker: A Study of His Theology* (London and New York, 1924).

Special studies

James D. G. Dunn, *Unity and Diversity in the New Testament* (Philadelphia, 1977).

Robert Hale, *Canterbury and Rome: Sister Churches* (New York, 1982).

Hans Küng and Walter Kasper (eds), *The Plurality of Ministries*, Concilium no. 74 (New York, 1972).

John Macquarrie, *Christian Unity and Christian Diversity* (London and Philadelphia, 1975).

John Macquarrie (ed.), *Realistic Reflections on Church Union* (Albany, N.Y., 1967).

Eric Mascall, *The Recovery of Unity: A Theological Approach* (London and New York, 1958).

Gerald Moede, *Oneness in Christ: The Quest and the Question*, Consultation on Church Union (Princeton, 1981).

A. M. Ramsey, *The Gospel and the Catholic Church* (London and New York, 1936).

Herbert J. Ryan and J. Robert Wright (eds.), *Episcopalians and Roman Catholics: Can They Ever Get Together?* (Denville, N.J., 1972).

Mark Santer (ed)., *Their Lord and Ours* (London, 1982).

Eduard Schweizer, *Church Order in the New Testament* (London, 1961).

Edward Schillebeeckx, *Ministry: A Case for Change* (London, 1981).

Additional documents

In Each Place: Towards a Fellowship of Local Churches Truly United, World Council of Churches (Geneva, 1977).

In Quest of a Church of Christ Uniting, revised edn., Consultation on Church Union (Princeton, 1980).

One Baptism, One Eucharist, and A Mutually Recognized Ministry: Three Agreed Statements, Faith and Order Paper no. 73, World Council of Churches (Geneva, 1975).

Index

115

117

118